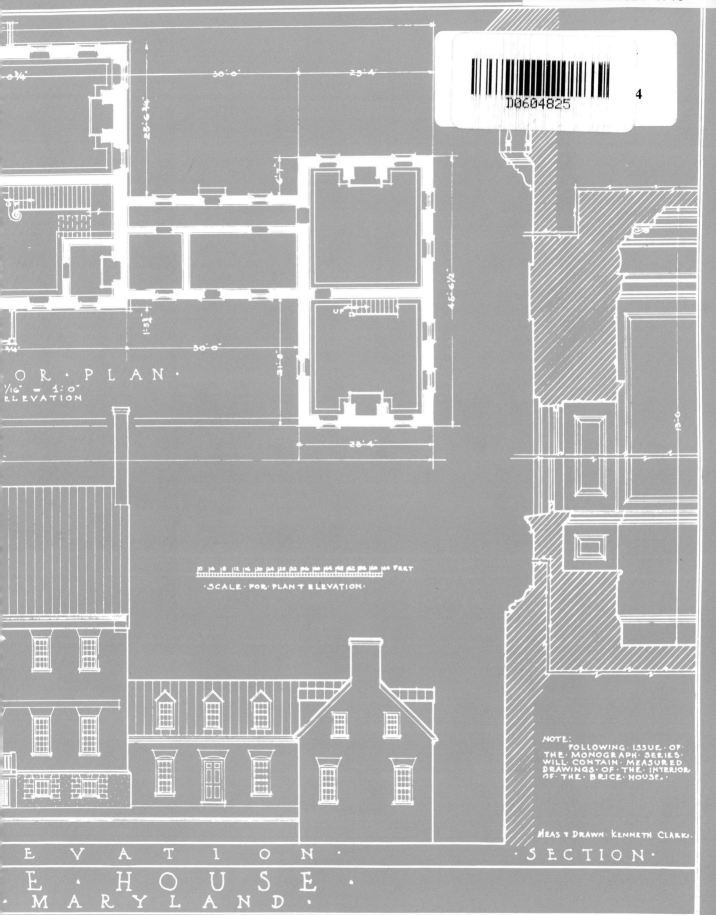

·OR·PLAN·

¹⁄₁₆" = 1:0"
ELEVATION

10 14 18 112 116 120 124 128 132 136 140 144 148 152 156 160 164 FEET
·SCALE·FOR·PLAN·+·ELEVATION·

NOTE:
FOLLOWING·ISSUE·OF·
THE·MONOGRAPH·SERIES·
WILL·CONTAIN·MEASURED·
DRAWINGS·OF·THE·INTERIOR·
OF·THE·BRICE·HOUSE·

MEAS·+·DRAWN·KENNETH·CLARK·

·E V A T I O N ·   · S E C T I O N ·

·E·HOUSE·

·M A R Y L A N D·

GRANDEUR OF
THE SOUTH

Other National Historical Society Publications:

THE IMAGE OF WAR: 1861–1865

TOUCHED BY FIRE: A PHOTOGRAPHIC PORTRAIT OF THE CIVIL WAR

WAR OF THE REBELLION: OFFICIAL RECORDS
  OF THE UNION AND CONFEDERATE ARMIES

OFFICIAL RECORDS OF THE UNION AND CONFEDERATE NAVIES
  IN THE WAR OF THE REBELLION

HISTORICAL TIMES ILLUSTRATED ENCYCLOPEDIA OF THE CIVIL WAR

A TRAVELLER'S GUIDE TO GREAT BRITAIN SERIES

For information about National Historical Society Publications, write:
Historical Times, Inc., 2245 Kohn Road, Box 8200, Harrisburg, Pennsylvania 17105

GRANDEUR OF THE SOUTH

From material originally published as
The Georgian Period
edited by
Professor William Rotch Ware

Lisa C. Mullins, Editor

Roy Underhill, Consultant

A Publication of
THE NATIONAL HISTORICAL SOCIETY

Library of Congress Cataloging-in-Publication Data

Grandeur of the South/Lisa C. Mullins, editor; Roy Underhill, consultant.
    (Architectural treasures of Early America; 14)
    1. Architecture, Georgian—South Carolina. 2. Architecture, Colonial—South Carolina. 3. Architecture—South Carolina. 4. Architecture, Georgian—Southern States. 5. Architecture, Colonial—Southern States. 6. Architecture—Southern States. I. Mullins, Lisa C. II. Series: Architectural treasures of Early America (Harrisburg, Pa.); 14.
NA730.S8G7 1988   720'.9757—dc19   88-1674
ISBN 0-918678-36-6

CONTENTS

HABS

"It was the best summer of my life! We would drive out to this great plantation every day and go to work. You learn so much about a building when you measure it — there are things that don't come out any other way. I learned what to look for in a house and how to spot the changes. It was neat. To have that kind of access to one of these really great houses was a real gas!"

Thousands of other people share architectural historian Mark R. Wenger's pleasant memories. Although his adventure happened in the 1970s, he was taking part in a program that began in the winter of the Great Depression. He was working for HABS, the Historic American Buildings Survey.

Charles Peterson came up with the idea in November of 1933. The Great Depression had put millions of people out of work. The Roosevelt administration was open to new ideas, and "nothing seemed too bold to try." Peterson proposed that unemployed architects be put to work recording all types of early American buildings. "It is the responsibility of the American people that if the great number of our antique buildings must disappear through economic cause, they shall not pass into unrecorded oblivion," Peterson said.

Architects had accumulated countless drawings in the preceding years, but they were often lost and were inaccessible to others. Much early architecture had also been recorded in such works as *The Georgian Period* and the *White Pine Series of Architectural Monographs,* usually to provide sources for Colonial Revival work, but there was no organized national survey. After 1930, when modern architecture began to take over, new books of measured drawings of early work ceased to appear. HABS took over at a critical juncture.

Recording buildings is a noble pursuit, but the purpose of the program was to put people back to work. Peterson projected that half a million dollars would employ a thousand architects. Many began work in that same winter of 1933. In regions where the need for employment relief was greatest, more positions were allocated, regardless of the number of sites that needed to be recorded. District officers throughout the nation had to decide which buildings would be recorded and assign their people appropriately. The district officer in charge of the survey in Alabama found that he had to schedule around delays caused by the extra time required to record the ornate ironwork in Mobile.

By the 1950s, the post-war building boom created a shortage of architects. Unlike most make-work projects of the New Deal, the work of HABS had proven so important that it had to continue, so HABS turned to students. For a college student to put his name on a set of drawings to be kept in the Library of Congress is quite an initiation. Their names joined the ranks of the greats of their profession. Architecture students of all sorts, not just those interested in historic work have taken part in this great work. At the end of the summer, there is often a party or picnic where everybody on the various teams from a region gets to meet one another. HABS has become "a family kind of thing."

HABS drawings are now on slightly larger sheets, and perhaps some of the modern drawings are less artistic, but considering how other things have changed over half a century, it remains an amazingly homogeneous set of information. The HABS people have very stringent standards, making sure that the drawings will literally overlay one another. The field workers record only what they see, not what they think used to be there. HABS wants an abstract, objective record for posterity. Other groups have very different ways of looking at buildings and recording them. They may ask, was this original? How has this changed? They may differentiate between a first period stud and a second period stud, but a HABS drawing will show all the studs the same, without comments or interpretation.

HABS is changing though. When Mark Wenger and his colleagues drew Westover, they were among the first permitted to use shading in their drawings of the chair rails, stair brackets, and ceiling plaster. Recently, when another HABS team drew Stratford Hall, they made an annotated set of drawings that included their findings on the evolution of the building. Photographs are also a big part of the HABS documenting process. Soon, perhaps, video and holography may join the paper and India ink.

HABS is jointly administered by the National Park Service, the American Institute of Architects and the Library of Congress, but it belongs to the people. All of the work of HABS is in the public domain and may be used by anyone in any way. The documents are indexed by geographic region and kept in the Prints and Photographs Reading Room of the Library of Congress. If you can not travel to Washington, many libraries have microfilm copies of the HABS collection. Individuals may also write to the Prints and Photographs Division of the Library of Congress to request a catalog and price list for reproductions. Or, you might want to join a HABS team in the field. The work goes on, and it just might turn out to be the best summer of your life.

ROY UNDERHILL
MASTER HOUSEWRIGHT
COLONIAL WILLIAMSBURG

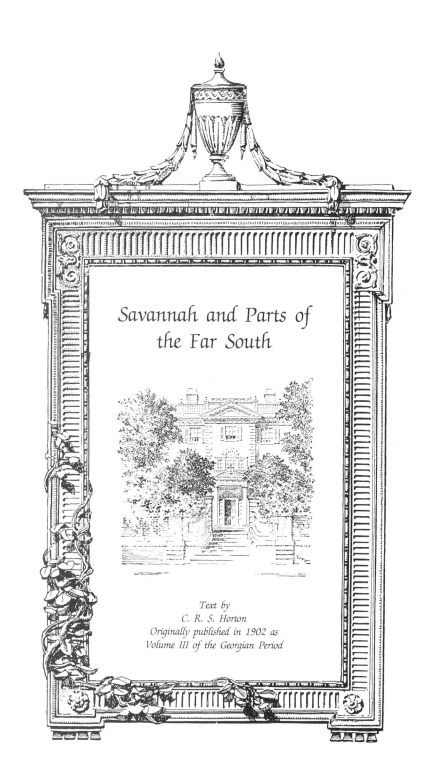

Savannah and Parts of
the Far South

Text by
C. R. S. Horton
Originally published in 1902 as
Volume III of the Georgian Period

Photograph by Mrs. Thaddeus Horton

GILMER HOUSE, BULL AND STATE STREETS, SAVANNAH, GEORGIA

SAVANNAH AND PARTS OF THE FAR SOUTH

THE student of Georgian architecture familiar with the Colonial work of New England, New York, the Genesee Valley and Virginia does not easily find interesting examples of the period farther south than Charleston and Beaufort, South Carolina. This may seem strange at first cry, but in reality it is what might be expected of a section of country developed for the most part late in the eighteenth century. Charleston, as is well known, was a fashionable community as early as 1773 with high ideas of art and architecture, with aristocratic tastes and manners. Beaufort and the neighboring sea islands were settled during the first part of the seventeenth century, and one of the earliest examples of good work in America is afforded by the Jenkins House on Edisto Island, which was built in 1683. Savannah, on the other hand, was a wilderness until 1733, when Oglethorpe landed with his party at Yamacraw Bluff. To the south of Savannah there was practically nothing in the way of civilization until about the beginning of the nineteenth century, except the Spanish settlement at St. Augustine, whence voyagers made their way along the coast, little by little, settling first in one spot and then another, which accounts for the strain of Spanish feeling which shows itself, as is obvious to any who take time to study the situation, through the region between Savannah and Florida. This reveals itself in the presence of low pavilion houses surrounded by one or two story verandas, between which and the characteristic houses of the Spanish West Indies and the quaint double-decked verandas of Charleston there is a strong analogy. New Orleans, to be sure, was settled about 1723 — a few years earlier than Savannah — and should afford good examples, but (unfortunately for those who are interested in English work and the many phases of its far-reaching influence) the early Louisianians were French and Spanish, and the architecture of the region proclaims the Latin rather than the Saxon.

Considering these facts it becomes apparent that the far South — Georgia, Alabama and Mississippi — was subject architecturally to the influences exerted by two different nationalities. The Georgian ideas of the English traveled south in company, naturally enough, with the early English settlers, who, as a class, being richer than the French Huguenots of the same period, built finer houses than the latter, thus exerting a more powerful influence architecturally. This influence may be said to have particularly affected the coast regions, whence it swept across the country, meeting finally a countercurrent from the West — the influence of the French and Spanish styles from New Orleans. Of these the English was destined to finally prove itself the most pronounced throughout the South; for, having acquired the habit of looking to the mother country for prototypes, the Southerner, always less violent in his antipathies to the English than his Northern brother, continued to do so after the Revolution, which accounts for the presence of the colonnaded house of the far South. This, strictly speaking, is an off-shoot from the Classic Revival which raged in England toward the last of the eighteenth century and first appeared on the east coast of America about 1800, whence, becoming immediately popular and being well adapted to the climate, it spread through the entire South from the Atlantic to the banks of the Mississippi and beyond them, enjoying a great popularity in the very heart of the French district. In fact, the white-columned house, despite its foreign origin, may be said to be more truly vernacular than anything in the South, for, in time, the ideas back of it became so absorbed by the Southern builder as to be almost a natural product resulting logically from the demands of climate and the tastes of the people.

Savannah, Georgia, though a seaport town of the colonial period, is strangely disappointing architecturally, and contains few specimens of any value, which is rather odd in view of the fact that, although the city was not settled until 1733, it had advanced far enough in the ethics of civilization by 1738 to hold balls and dinners in honor of distinguished English visitors

OLD EXCHANGE — 1799 — SAVANNAH, GEORGIA

From the Harbor
OLD EXCHANGE BUILDING, SAVANNAH, GEORGIA

From the Land
OLD EXCHANGE BUILDING, SAVANNAH, GEORGIA

OLD BRICK TOMB, SAVANNAH, GEORGIA

and of those who were continually coming over from Charleston to have a hand in the management of things and to acquire for themselves and their heirs landed interests of one kind or another in the new colony.

In fact, though entirely different in exterior aspect, Savannah is redolent with suggestions of the Carolinas, especially of Charleston. There is Bull Street, named for Col. William Bull, of Carolina, who laid out the city of Savannah. There is Drayton Street, named for Thomas Drayton, of the Ashley River, and St. Julian Street, called for James St. Julian, a friend of the Georgia colonists; and, although the Savannah houses for the most part belong to a later period than the interesting old dwellings pictured in earlier pages as representing the architecture of Charleston, the observer is constantly running upon, unawares, old Georgian doorways set in the plainest of clapboarded houses, fanlights, bits of old ironwork: all of which remind one that ideas once cast abroad are continually cropping up in fertile places. The paucity of early work in Savannah may be due to two different causes, first, that two fires swept the city, the last as late as 1802; second, that aside from General Oglethorpe and his

party, which included the rich immigrants, colonial Georgia was more an asylum for those who sought to prove that poverty was no disgrace than for those favored ones of fortune interested in building fine houses.

The oldest structure of any consequence in Savannah today is the Exchange Building, which, begun in 1799, has filled a variety of functions for over a century, having been as often used as a theatre, a ballroom, and a place of general assembly on patriotic occasions as for commercial purposes.

Next to the Exchange Building the oldest and perhaps the most interesting pieces of work in Savannah are four residences which were built about the same time by the same architect and may therefore be classed together.

These are commonly spoken of as Scarborough House, which is situated in Yamacraw, the oldest section of the city; Owens House, the Telfair residence, now the Telfair Art Gallery, and Bulloch House on Orleans Square.

All of these houses were built by an English architect by the name of Jay who did considerable work in and around Savannah early in the nineteenth century.

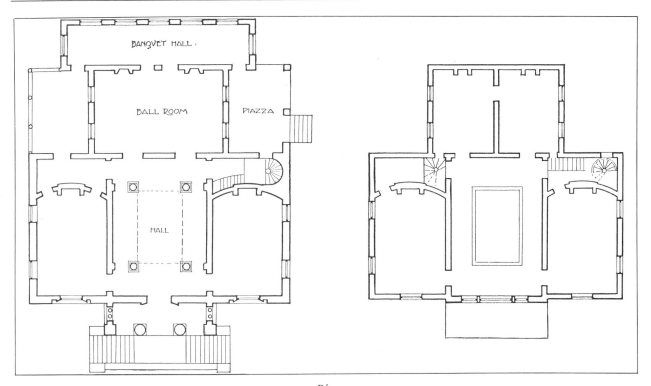

Plan

SCARBOROUGH HOUSE, BROAD STREET, SAVANNAH

The Owens House is known to have been built in 1815, the Bulloch House was completed in 1818 and the other two about the same period. The Owens House, strange to say, is built of "tabby,"[1] which must have been a material new to the English architect; the others are of brick sent from England presumably, although native brick was procurable in Savannah as early as 1820. The Owens, the Telfair, and the Scarborough houses are not dissimilar though they are quite differently proportioned, and may be said to express, in a vague way the architectural personality of the builder. Of the three the Scarborough House is the most interesting. Though at present utilized as a negro school and situated in the heart of a rough district, robbed of all interior adornment, marred by the elements, and deprived by chance of the quiet and repose to which in the natural order of things old places seem entitled, it possesses still, though given up to vulgar usage, a singular air of repose and dignity.

All of the houses built by Jay in Savannah were square in plan, with kitchen and servants' rooms in an ell to the rear. All of the rooms were large, the feature of each house being invariably the staircase, which

in each of these four instances was constructed differently. In the case of the Scarborough House the staircase, which is exceedingly wide and of a rather heavy design, rises abruptly immediately in front of the entrance, leaving an open space to the rear of it; the Telfair staircase rises in very much the same manner, but is constructed differently; the staircase of the Owens House rises about the middle center of the hallway to the rear of a colonnade consisting of four gold-capped Corinthian columns, and ascends to a landing, on either side of which second runs arise completing the ascent to the story above, the stair-opening

Photograph by Mrs. Thaddeus Horton.

SCARBOROUGH HOUSE — 1815 — BROAD
STREET, SAVANNAH

Jay, Architect

---

[1] "Tabby" is evidently a corruption of the Spanish "*tapia*," a mud wall, and the material is a species of concrete or artificial stone composed largely of pounded oystershells. The tabby-built house of South Carolina and Georgia must not be confounded with the houses built in Florida of coquina, a natural limestone with marine shells and coral for the conglomerate. — WARE

BELLE GROVE, IBERVILLE PARISH, LOUISIANA

BELLE GROVE, IBERVILLE PARISH, LOUISIANA

Photograph by Mrs. Thaddeus Horton

TELFAIR ART GALLERY — c1815–1820 — SAVANNAH

Jay, Architect

thus made forming a sort of arcade through which those on the upper story can see what is going on below. The staircase of the Bulloch House is spiral in character.

Although the city of Savannah is disappointing in itself to those interested in searching out specimens of the early work of American builders, the surrounding country, if studied understandingly, offers many interesting suggestions in the way of country-houses which point to that mode of life peculiar to the far South prior to the Civil War. One of the best of these is the Hermitage, on a rice plantation on the Savannah River, six miles or so out from the city, which though not built until about 1820, is interesting, inasmuch as the materials used in its construction were chiefly native bricks which are known to have been manufactured on the spot; and furthermore in that it has preserved to this day the quaint negro cabins and quarters that were in use during slavery, the place as a whole having been but lightly touched by the hand of those given to modern improvements.

It is curiously interesting during these days which, even in the South, are so far removed in spirit from the days of half a century ago to find oneself surrounded by the symbols of a life which to modern eyes is curiously unlike anything now existing. Passing up the wide sandy road that leads to the Hermitage, bordered on either side with giant water-oaks overgrown with tillandsia (Spanish moss), one sees the brick mansion itself at the end of a vista of misty, swaying drapery, flanked to the front (or rear, whichever you prefer, the Hermitage having two fronts, one facing the river and the other the land road) with parallel rows of negro huts, some of brick, others of wood, and still others of tabby, having, as a rule, thatched roofs. There, too, is the slave hospital, an unusual-looking pavilionlike structure smacking of the West Indies. Little by little the slave quarters of the Hermitage have fallen into

hopeless disrepair; but enough remains even at this late day to interest, not only students of American civilization, but even the casual observer, who, as a rule, is not susceptible to historical impressions. The Hermitage produces an indescribable sensation. The house, though more or less Georgian in character, with a tendency toward such thoughtful work as could be produced in that locality at that period, represents on the whole a later epoch than the buildings we have been considering. It also represents a civilization later than that of the colonial period. Nevertheless, the place, as a whole, surrounded, as it is, with slave huts, beyond which stretch the low, level rice and cotton fields, through which the broad Savannah River wanders at pleasure, dawdling here and hurrying there, stands for a mode of life more typical of the south of the United States than any of the more formal abodes of a more formal people.

The civilization of Charleston prior to the Revolution as well as that of Salem, Massachusetts, and the other coast cities of the colonies, was practically English, just as the life that obtains today in the "British Dominions Beyond the Sea" reflects the ideas and ideals of the mother country; but the civilization that arose in the far South after the Revolution was of another *genre*. This is particularly true of the rice-plantation district, and the Cotton, or "black," Belt, which began in the central part of Western Georgia and stretched across Alabama, Mississippi, and a part of Louisiana, in which, prior to the war, the greatest number of negroes were congested, their presence being a necessary adjunct of the successful production of the vast crops of the region. Each of the world's great staples creates a life peculiar to itself to which those who handle it are subject, and, as a natural result, existence in the rice regions of South Carolina and Georgia and in the Cotton Belt, though colored,

Photograph by Mrs. Thaddeus Horton

MINUS HOUSE, ORLEANS SQUARE, SAVANNAH

Photograph by Mrs. Thaddeus Horton

OWENS HOUSE — 1815 — SAVANNAH

Jay, Architect

it is true, by English and French influences, so adapted itself to the climate and to the large, yet simple, demands of plantation duties as to produce something similar yet different, something altogether American, colored and modified by the gentle genius of the Southern country. The region between Savannah and Brunswick, around about Darien, and up and down the Altamaha River, comprised the richest rice-lands in Georgia, stocked with game—wild duck, wild turkey, snipe, woodcock, rice-birds—shaded with live-oak and cypress trees, and dotted here and there with green marshes. These regions exhibit a great variety of plantation-houses possessing no architectural features, being for the most part mere carpenter shacks, yet so obviously the result of human existence and its needs, of demand and supply, as to be valuable as types. It is strange how a house with no architectural enrichment, with no architectural grammar, so to speak, may yet possess a certain charm, a certain original value of its own. The art of building, always so closely allied to the many phases of human life, is never more obviously so than in the plantation districts of the far South, and there one sometimes comes upon original ideas of construction, crudely expressed, but interesting, and often significant.

One of the celebrated plantations of the Altamaha region was formerly owned by Pierce Butler, whose marriage with Fanny Kemble was one of the notable events of the early 1830s, and it was while spending a winter at this place that the actress wrote her celebrated *Journal of Life on a Georgia Plantation,* which was published some years later and widely read both in this country and England. The house on the Butler estate is no longer standing, having been a poor thing, somewhat after the bungalow style, built by the crudest of slave labor.

Perhaps the most pretentious piece of work on the Altamaha was Hopeton House, the place of James

Hamilton Couper, who, in common with Pierce Butler, had large holdings in this section as well as on the sea islands which hug the coast of Georgia and produce as fine sea-island cotton as the world affords. Hopeton House is now a ruin, but from sketches of it preserved in the Couper family it appears to have been after the style of an English manor house. The plans of Hopeton House were drawn by Mr. Couper himself, and the building operations were conducted under his supervision, for, in common with many Southern gentlemen of that period, he was a student of architecture and a liberal subscriber to English periodicals and plates.[2] Another example of his work is afforded by Christ Church, Savannah, built about 1838, which, though rather commercial in character, is perhaps the most interesting of the Savannah churches.

Hopeton was the scene of a very fashionable and elaborate winter life from the early 1830s until the late 1850s, and guests from all parts of America and abroad were entertained there after the hospitable style of the Southern planter; that life that obtained there being, on the whole, not dissimilar from the life that is considered peculiar to the country gentry of England, with the exception that the crop was cultivated by black slaves instead of by white tenantry. Indeed Mr. Couper made an effort to adopt the English tenantry plan in its entirety,[3] but the negro character proved too shiftless to be entirely entrusted with the management of land. One of the many notable guests entertained at Hopeton during the early 1850s was the Honorable Amelia M. Murray, an English litterateur and Court lady, who, while touring the United States and Canada, wrote her impressions in letters to England, which were published in one of the London papers and afterwards brought out in book form. While at Hopeton she enjoyed her first intimate view of Southern plantation life, and was so favorably impressed

[2] Voluminous works on architecture and folio-plates are to be found in many old Southern libraries.

[3] Writes the Hon. Amelia Murray in her letters: "Mr. Couper tells me he once tried the capabilities of the most active among his people by giving them the cultivation of fifty acres for themselves; the first season, under direction, the plantation cleared $1,500, which he took care to give to them in silver, hoping that would incite their industry; the next year he left to their own management; the crop lessened one-half; and the third season, left to themselves, they let the land run to waste so that it was useless to let them retain it. Yet these same people will labor readily and contentedly under good superintendence. And such is their feeling for their master that in some cases where freshets have put his crops in danger they have worked freely eighteen hours out of the twenty-four to save them—more than they would have done for themselves in any such case. The thanks of Mr. Couper and a few little presents made them quite happy. They are devoted servants and miserable free people. When I watch the consideration, kindness and patience shown by the white gentlemen and white gentlewoman to these darkies, I could say to some antislavery people I have known, 'Go thou and do likewise.'"

THE HERMITAGE, ON THE SAVANNAH RIVER, GEORGIA

JAMES K. POLK MANSION, NASHVILLE, TENNESSEE

BULLOCH HOUSE—1818—ORLEANS SQUARE,
SAVANNAH

Jay, Architect

with it and the happy and healthy condition of Mr. Couper's four hundred slaves that she wrote in vindication of slavery in the South, to which, as is well known, the British masses were greatly opposed. Her letters naturally excited the displeasure and condemnation of the English people, who had preconceived opinions on the subject which they did not care to relinquish. In one of them[4] she compared the state of the Southern negro slave to that of the Scotch and Irish peasant classes, and so unfavorably to the latter that the British public, already displeased, became so highly incensed that Mrs. Murray's dismissal from Court became necessary as an act of policy. It is interesting to know that two such contrary reports as those of the Honorable Mrs. Murray and of Frances Ann Kemble could have emanated respectively from two Englishwomen viewing the same locality at almost the same period.

The fact that the plantation districts of the far South, those stretching through the interior of Georgia, Alabama, the western part of South Carolina, and the central portion of Mississippi and the northern portion of Florida were settled for the most part about the first of the nineteenth century removes the work of that region from what is, properly speaking, the Georgian period; yet the presence of the white-colonnaded

houses throughout this section shows plainly that the architectural influence of England continued after the Revolution. This is more particularly true of the South, beginning with Virginia, than with the North, although one of the earliest and best examples of a colonnaded portico in America is the Childs House, Rochester, New York, built in 1800. The colonnaded house of the far South, which, in its degenerate form, may be spoken of as the "white-pillared" house, does not belong to the Georgian period, but to the Classic Revival, which was, however, so obviously an outgrowth of preceding styles as to come in naturally for some consideration; furthermore, the white-pillared house is, in a sense, the final figure in the background upon which our present architectural modernity rests.

But for the Greek Revival which started in England toward the last of the eighteenth century, the general character of architectural styles in the plantation districts of the far South would have been quite different, though one can but wonder what the Southern planter would have built on his savanna had not Greek and Roman columns been dominant in the work of the day. Certainly nothing could have more perfectly suited his climate, the large yet simple purposes of his life, or his taste, which, as a rule, was more or less grandiose. One must have a portico in the South. Why not have it extend all around the house? One must have posts to support the roof of the portico. Why not have Greek columns instead (since they were the fashion)? The proposition was beautifully simple; so sim-

---

[4] "I forgot to mention," writes Mrs. Murray, "that there are from three to four hundred negroes on this estate. Mr. and Mrs. Couper have no white servants; their family consists of six sons and three daughters. I should not like to inhabit a lonely part of Ireland or even Scotland surrounded only by three hundred Celts. I believe there is not a solider or policeman nearer than Savannah, a distance of sixty miles. Surely this speaks volumes for the contentment of the slave population. When I think of the misery and barbarism of the peasantry in Kintail and other parts of Scotland (putting aside that of Ireland) and then look at the people here it is hardly possible not to blush at the recollection of all the hard words I have heard applied to the slaveholders of the South. Why, the very pigsties of the negroes are better than some Celtic hovels I have seen."

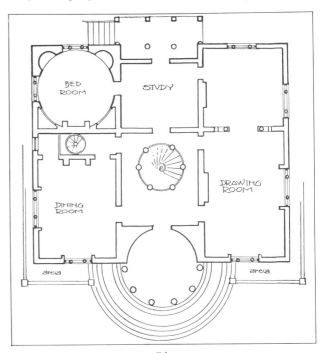

Plan

BULLOCH HOUSE, ORLEANS SQUARE, SAVANNAH

Portico
BULLOCH HOUSE, SAVANNAH, GEORGIA

to the Capitol. The White House, by the way, though it did not take on its Ionic portico until about 1820, when, during the administration of Andrew Jackson, it was remodeled, is one of the most notable examples of the Classic Revival in America, and on the whole, a typical residence of an English country gentleman — our presidents of the early nineteenth century were American country gentlemen.

Andrew Jackson may have had some influence in deciding on the character of the improvements, for, as is well known, he was himself a great admirer of the Classic Orders, and The Hermitage, his seat near Nashville, shows a white colonnade.

Fort Hill,[5] the seat of John C. Calhoun, which was built early in the nineteenth century after designs drawn by Calhoun himself, was another effort to follow the style most approved in England. It is, on the whole, a poor structure, built of local material and by untrained slave labor, yet the front portico with its columns of solid masonry is rather imposing. You can

[5] Fort Hill (c1902) is now the property of Clemson College, of which it is a part.

Drawing Room
BULLOCH HOUSE, SAVANNAH, GEORGIA

ple, indeed, that, once introduced, the style spread with remarkable rapidity. The grandeur of the effect and the simplicity with which it was obtained were both in its favor. The more columns the Southern planter used the better he liked it; and, since one was copying Greek styles, why not copy the Temple of Theseus or the Parthenon and be done with it? The Southern planter of the early nineteenth century was a man of enormous purposes; the architectural ideas suggested by the greatest monuments of antiquity were but grist for his mill, and, as a result, full half the houses in the South — the Coleman House, of Macon, Georgia, the Pew House in Madison, Dunleith, in Natchez (the mansard roof of which is a late addition), Houmas house, on the Mississippi, Belle Grove, also on the Mississippi, and many others, were all expressions, in one form or another, of the same idea.

At the time when the Greek Revival was at its height in England, the United States was just beginning to recover from the ravages of the Revolution and to turn its attention toward building. The government let a contract for the White House, and for additions

Stairway
BULLOCH HOUSE — 1830 — SAVANNAH, GEORGIA

Photograph by Mrs. Thaddeus Horton

Portico
McALPIN HOUSE — c1820 — ORLEANS SQUARE,
SAVANNAH, GEORGIA

make white columns absurd, but, try as you will, you can't make them *very* ugly. The art gallery opens to one side on another columned portico which leads out across a flagged floor to the level of the lawn. The library is a separate building — a not uncommon arrangement in the South — which allowed its use as an office as well. The interior of Fort Hill shows a succession of rather low rooms opening into one another, reached through unexpected passages, which indicates that the house was added to from time to time rather than that it was built originally as it now stands. At the time of the death of its last individual owner, Clemson, Calhoun's son-in-law, Fort Hill was very much as it had been during the statesman's lifetime. It was filled with curious furniture, pictures, china, and the walls showed the quaint paperings of a past period. The library was filled with old editions and newspapers, old manuscripts, and dusty scrapbooks

showing press comments upon the period when Clay, Calhoun and Webster swayed the country with their great controversies and splendid eloquence. The art gallery was hung with family portraits, and, as a whole, Fort Hill presented as complete a setting for the home life of a great man of the middle nineteenth century as could be found in America.

In considering the influences exerted by the styles of the Greek Revival, it is necessary to divide the white-columned houses of the South into two groups — those built by professional architects and those built by the owners themselves. Of the two, the latter were in the great majority. In fact, almost the only white-columned houses showing the touch of the student's hand are those found occasionally in the coast cities of the South. One of the earliest of these is the Witte House, of Charleston. This, as explained elsewhere, was built in 1810 after designs furnished by English architects, and is, on the whole, a very ambitious piece of building, more European than American in character. Although a town house, it enjoys all the advantages of privacy in a remarkable degree, for while the front overlooks an English garden and aviary, the rear is built up on a line with the side street that marks the city block, affording a tradesmen's entrance and the other conveniences necessary. Passing along this street and looking up at the pretentious four-story structure from the rear, one would imagine it but an ordinary city residence, while in reality, like a true mystic, it hides its beauties from view. By adroit arrangement often seen in European cities it turns its *worst* side to the public, saving its abundant adornment for those who know and love it intimately. The Andrum House, with its lofty pillared portico to one side, is another Charleston example of the influence of the Greek Revival.

The Bulloch House, Savannah, Georgia, which was built in 1818, is, on the whole, a pretentious piece of work. It was designed by Jay and built, according to tradition, of English brick.

With such houses as these as models the Southern planter of the early nineteenth century began his task, which was a large one. Usually he had two houses to build, one on his plantation and another in some neighboring village for the convenience of his family; consequently, such towns as Athens, Washington and La Grange, Georgia, Greenwood, Alabama, Aberdeen, Mississippi, and others of the same class, filled with white-pillared houses of one kind or another (for the Southerner, having become accustomed to this style, was satisfied with no other), spring up through the Cotton Belt, and maintained their unruffled existence until the breaking out of the Civil War.

The building of a village house and a country-house

THE HERMITAGE, NASHVILLE, TENNESSEE

THE HERMITAGE, ON THE SAVANNAH RIVER, GEORGIA

McALPIN HOUSE, ORLEANS SQUARE,
SAVANNAH, GEORGIA

the rear as well), with the kitchen occupying a low pavilion to one side.[6]

Having perfected his plans the Southern planter set about having them executed. Bands of negroes searched the uncleared lands for suitable timber. Trees were often used for columns, when those of the required proportions could be secured, and if flutes were desired they were cut out by hand (time was of no consideration in the Cotton Belt). Foliated capitals of one kind or another were occasionally used when a workman could be found who could execute so delicate a task; but until then years or so before the Civil War, when galvanized capitals first made their appearance, the Doric order only was attempted in the Cotton Belt. Most commonly, however, the columns were made of masonry, rough-cast, as in the case of the Hansell House, at Roswell, Georgia; sometimes they were built square, with a Byzantine effect; and occasionally they were crude constructions of long, dressed plank put together in sections, as in the case of the Bulloch House, at Roswell, built about 1820.

Working under such disadvantages it is not surprising that some of the houses of Southern builders thus planned and executed were, as might be expected, pathetic objects, with enormous porticos out of all proportion to the importance of the house into which they afford entrance, reminding one eternally of such ambitious persons as invariably put their best foot forward. In the South, as elsewhere, man was not master of his fate in architecture, and often houses, even those most carefully planned, the proportions of whose columns were most carefully studied, worked out their own untoward end, just as a child sometimes achieves a sad destiny independent of its parent.

were two entirely different propositions, the former being comparatively easy, as material was procurable with little difficulty; but the planter, clearing a new plantation, and building a covering from himself here and there throughout the vast unexplored Southern wilderness, just after the Revolution and at the beginning of the nineteenth century, was facing the enormous task which from time immemorial has confronted migratory man. First, of course, he built a hut, then he added to it, then after a few years, when his land began yielding plentifully, he turned himself to the building of a permanent domicile. By this time white columns were to be seen in the South. Perhaps he built a one-story house, in which event the white columns were usually there just the same, or, perhaps, the plantation being near enough to civilization for his family to reside there all the year round, he prepared careful plans, with four great rooms to a floor—two on each side, with a wide hallway running between—and a two-storied portico to the front (and sometimes to

---

[6] See drawing of Calhoun House, Newnan, Georgia. The Calhoun House, at Newnan, has two fronts, one a reproduction of the other. The story told and generally credited in connection with this fact is to the effect that the builder and his wife disagreed as to whether the open expanse in front of the house should be utilized as a lawn or a flower garden. It proved impossible to settle this matter amicably until Mr. Calhoun conceived the happy idea of allowing the house to have two fronts and repeated in the rear the colonnade treatment intended for the front. As a result the Calhoun House faces a grove of trees on one side, and a terraced flower garden on the other. This arrangement forced the kitchen into a side ell which otherwise might have extended to the rear. The kitchen in the far South prior to the Civil War was most commonly an entirely separate outbuilding, situated at a distance of 50 or 100 feet from the house, sometimes reached by a covered passageway, but just as often not. When placed in an ell they were invariably separated from the body of the house by a covered veranda. Such an arrangement seems an awkward one in face of present day usages, but servants being plentiful in the South prior to the War, no thought was given to their convenience. A very distinguished lady who in her youth lived in the Drayton-Gibbes House, Charleston, tells me that quite often breakfast was served in the drawing room, which occupied one side of the third floor. (Think of having a drawing room on the third floor!) "And," she says, "when we wanted a hot waffle the steward had to run down two flights of stairs and out in the yard to get it."

HANSELL HOUSE—1820—ROSEWELL, GEORGIA

BULLOCH HOUSE—1820—ROSEWELL, GEORGIA

Others just as unexpectedly developed into true architecture, unions of tradition and necessity in beauty. For all that, however, the white-columned house fulfilled its functions perfectly—which is always the main consideration. So perfectly that after thirty-five years' experience with other styles the rich Southerner has found nothing that so perfectly suits him; and as a result many modern houses of today in the South are repeating the colonnade and other features of the antebellum residence. In time the old and the new may possibly stand as the accepted architecture of the far South, where climatic conditions are absolutely opposed to the small windows, low ceilings, and compressed styles acceptable elsewhere.

One of the features that particularly distinguish the Southern residence from its Northern contemporary is the presence of the veranda, which, brought to the South from the West Indies, whence it had traveled from Spain, Italy, and even from England (there were tavern verandas and balconies during Will Shakespear's day), developed many new and interesting phases in the hands of the Southern planter. First, there is the porch of the Georgian period, well illustrated by the Miles Brewton House of Charleston; then there is the huge three and four story verandas of the San Domingo houses of Charleston, presenting a form of construction that is continually reproducing itself throughout the far South; finally, there is the colonnade veranda of the white-pillared houses of the Cotton Belt.

With these three *motifs* to work with, the Southern builder, limited as he was in material and labor (for though slave labor was plentiful it was always unskilled during this early phase of Southern life), produced many varieties of shaded retreats.

A section of country which affords an interesting exhibit of country-houses, well adapted to a semi-

Photograph by Mrs. Thaddeus Horton
Portico
THE HERMITAGE—1830—ON THE SAVANNAH
RIVER, GEORGIA

INDEPENDENT PRESBYTERIAN CHURCH,
SAVANNAH, GEORGIA

The present church, of white marble, built not many
years ago, is an exact reproduction of the one
burned shortly before.

the whole were better suited to a warm climate than
French ones, which belong to a higher latitude) as to
be similar in much to the Hispano-English houses of
Charleston and the surrounding country.

It is this feeling—the Spanish feeling—which con-
nects the low pavilion houses of the French parishes
with the work we have been considering; it is this
influence—the Spanish influence—which blends the
east of the far South with the west of the far South,
together with what is to be found on the Mississippi
River representing with some picturesqueness the
architectural ideas of the Greek Revival.

Natchez, on the Mississippi, which was first settled
about 1720, was, prior to the war, a typical city of the
Cotton and Sugar Belt, and many of its old homes are
still intact, notably Dunleith and Montebello, which
may be said to stand for the Classic Revival in its most
pronounced form, as adapted to plantation conditions
in the far South.

All along the Mississippi, from Natchez through the
connecting parishes with their quaint pavilion houses,
White Ladies, Les Chênes, Plaisance Plantation, and
many other celebrated homes of old Creole families,
to New Orleans, one finds still many buildings and
customs that point clearly enough to the life of the old
seigneurs. In Lower Mississippi the signs of a similar
civilization are to be found. Beauvoir, the home of
Jefferson Davis, is typical of the houses of this region.
It is surrounded by detached pavilions, one used as a
library, another used for the exclusive accommodation
of gentlemen guests, and as a whole, simple, cool,
spacious, it is a representative abode of a Southern
country gentleman of that section of country.

A guest visiting the plantation homes of Lower
Mississippi or in the parishes is still given a cup of
black coffee and a roll in the early morning; then he is
invited to accompany his host on horseback to inspect
the crops. On their return breakfast is served—a meal
of real French abundance and variety, accompanied by
a display of fine china and linen, and tall bottles of
Bordeaux—offered with a kindliness and courtesy not
to be exceeded, and enjoyed to the accompaniment of
animated small talk.

tropical climate, is that part of Louisiana given up to
the Catholic parishes and inhabited almost exclusively
by French Creoles. These parishes, settled originally by
French-Canadian immigrants, stretch from the Gulf
and Bay of Biloxi as far north as Natchez, Mississippi.
As the residence section of what was formerly a colony
of French Catholics, the houses still standing in these
parishes are naturally Gallic in character, and yet so
strongly influenced by Spanish ideas as well (which on

BELMONT, LOUDON COUNTY, VIRGINIA

SAFFORD HOMESTEAD, NEAR MADISON, GEORGIA

HOUSE OF JUDGE REUBEN DAVIS, ABERDEEN, MISSIS

THE CALHOUN HOMESTEAD, NEWNAN, GEORGIA

LEYDON HOUSE, ATLANTA, GEORGIA

ASTRUDEVILLE, VIRGINIA

J. C. CALHOUN H
SOU

NEW ORLEANS BARRACKS, NEW ORLEANS, LOUISIANA

URSULINE CONVENT, NEW ORLEANS, LOUISIANA

WINDY HILL, NEAR NATCHEZ, MISSISSIPPI

ARCHBISHOP'S PALACE, NEW ORLEANS

URSULINE CONVENT, NEW ORLEANS, LOUISIANA

St. Michael's and St. Philip's

Text by
C. R. S. Horton
Originally published in 1902 as
Volume III of the Georgian Period

ST. MICHAEL'S CHURCH, CHARLESTON, SOUTH CAROLINA

ST. MICHAEL'S AND ST. PHILIP'S, CHARLESTON, SOUTH CAROLINA

ST. Michael's, the second home of the Church of England in Charleston, was erected on the site of the first St. Philip's, which, for the second time, outgrew itself by 1751. This necessitated the founding of a new parish, to which end an act was passed, in part, as follows: "That all that part of Charleston, situated and lying to the southward of the middle of Broad Street . . . be known by the name of the Parish of St. Michael's," and that a church be erected "on or near the spot where the old church of St. Philip's, Charleston, formerly stood," at a cost to the public of not more than 17,000 pounds, proclamation money.[1]

The church erected under this act still stands, an enduring monument to the architectural ideas and taste of old Charleston, and is famous not only for its historic associations, but also for its antique chime of bells. At the evacuation of Charleston, 1782, Major Traille, of the Royal Artillery, took down the bells of St. Michael's Church under the pretense that they were a military perquisite belonging to the commanding officer of artillery. The Vestry sought in vain to have them returned. They finally appealed to Sir Guy Carleton at New York, April 28, 1783. He issued an immediate order for their return together with all other public or private property of the inhabitants that may have been brought away. The bells, however, had been shipped from Charleston to London, where they were sold. The Vestry applied to the Minister of War of Great Britain, but in vain. The bells were finally purchased by a private individual, who returned them to Charleston as a gift, November, 1783. St. Michael's was opened for Divine service on February 1, 1761, six years earlier than Christ Church, Alexandria, Virginia, where Washington worshipped.

The cornerstone of St. Michael's was laid February 17, 1752, by Governor Glenn, and concerning this ceremony the *Charleston Gazette* of February 22 of that year speaks as follows: —

"The Commissioners for the building of the Church of St. Michael's of this town, having waited on His Excellency, the Governor, to desire that he would please lay the first stone, on Monday last, His Excellency, attended by several of His Majesty's Honorable Council, with the Commissioners, and other gentlemen, was pleased to proceed to the spot and lay the same, and accordingly, and therefor a sum of money a stone was then laid by each of the gentlemen who attended His Excellency, followed by a loud acclamation of a numerous concourse of people that had assembled to see the ceremony; after which the company proceeded to Mr. Gordon's, where a handsome entertainment was provided by the Commissioners."

The bill for this "handsome entertainment" is still

---

[1] "Proclamation money, which is also frequently mentioned in our Acts of Assembly, acquired that denomination from a proclamation of Queen Ann in the sixth year of her reign, about the year 1708: the object of which was to establish a common measure of value for the paper currencies of the Colonies. . . . The standard fixed by the proclamation, was, one hundred and thirty-three pounds, six shillings and eight pence (133. 6. 8.) paper currency, for one hundred pounds sterling. The dollar passed at six shillings and three pence." — *Brevard's Alphabetical Digest of the Public Laws of South Carolina.*

". . . the confusion arising from the different values of British sterling and provincial paper money, became general throughout the Colonies. In some a dollar passed for six shillings, in others for seven and sixpence, in North Carolina and New York for eight shillings, in South Carolina for one pound twelve shillings and sixpence. In the latter, the comparative value of sterling coin and paper money diverged so far from each other that after passing through all the intermediate grades of depreciation, it was finally fixed at seven pounds of the paper money for one pound sterling." — *Dr. Ramsay, History of South Carolina, Vol. I, p. 163.*

preserved in the archives of the church and reads as follows: —

Feb. 17, 1761. The Commissioners of the Church Bill.

To Dinner	£20
To Toddy	5, 10, 0
To Punch	5, 0, 0
To Beer	5, 10, 0
To Wine	5, 5, 0
To Glass broak	5, 0
To 8 magnum bonums of claret	0, 0
	£65, 10,

To this in a different hand is added "The Commissioners agree that the clerk pay this account." There is, however, no mention of this in the *Gazette's* account of the ceremony, which continues as follows: —

"Dinner over, His Majesty's health was drunk, followed by a discharge of the cannon at Granville's Bastion; then the health of the royal family and other loyal toasts, and the day was concluded with peculiar pleasure and satisfaction. The church will be built on the plan of one of Mr. Gibson's designs, and it is thought will exhibit a fine piece of architecture when completed, the steeple being designed much higher than that of St. Philip's [the second St. Philip's] will have a fine set of bells."

Although in this extract no mention is made of the location of the cornerstone, it is stated in an old memorandum-book belonging to the church that "on this day the Governor laid the first stone on the southeast corner of the church." Following this information a search was made for the cornerstone at the time when extensive repairs, made necessary by the earthquake, were under way, but without success. An interesting discovery was made, however, to the effect that the steeple was built on a foundation entirely separate from that on which the body of the church rested.

St. Michael's has been very generally considered the work of an architect by the name of Gibson, said to be a pupil of Sir Christopher Wren's, but a clever writer on the subject in the *Charleston Year Book* of 1886 seeks to prove otherwise. He says: "The name of the architect is given as Gibson, a name of which we can find no mention elsewhere; but James Gibbs was the designer of St. Martin's-in-the-Fields, London; and a legend tells us that our church is a copy of that building. A glance at the pictures of the two shows this to be an error, and one is puzzled to account for the story. If, however, they were planned by the same person, we can see how the error arose. Add to this the similarity of Gibbs and Gibson, and the fact that the spires of both churches spring through the roof; and the further fact that Gibbs lived until 1754, and we

think there is little doubt that St. Michael's was the work of Gibbs. This, however, is as each man pleases."

Exactly who built St. Michael's may never be known. The old church stands unchanged by time, with the golden ball of its spire[2] to be seen from the fishing boats far out at sea; with its quiet graves about it, enclosed by a high brick wall, to which the people pass through two great iron gates said to be the work of A. Iusti, who at one time lived in Charleston, and together with Deidrick Werner, a German, is responsible for much that is most artistic in the wrought ironwork of the city. Service is held in St. Michael's regularly; and in the quaint old pews, to which the floors have been raised to render them less box-like than formerly, sit the descendants of those who composed its original congregation. Generations, young and old, have passed beneath its portals, and its sweet chimes have carried, and still carry, balm and comfort to thousands of hearts.

Mr. Dalcho gives the following description of St. Michael's in his *Church History of South Carolina* published in 1819: —

"It is of brick and is rough cast. The extreme length of the building is 130 feet, and it is 60 feet wide. The nave is 74 feet wide, the chancel, 10, the vestibule inside, 22, and the portico, 16. It contains ninety-three pews on the ground floor, the middle aisle across the church having lately been built up with eight new pews, and forty-five in the gallery. The chancel is handsome, and is ornamented in the most appropriate manner. It is a panelled wainscot, with four Corinthian pilasters supporting the proper cornice. The usual tables of the Decalogue, Apostles' Creed and Lord's Prayer are placed between them. The galleries are supported by twelve Ionic pillars. The reading-desk and pulpit stand at the east end of the church. Near the middle door stands a handsome marble font of an oval form. The ceiling is flat, ornamented with a rich cornice, which runs nearly parallel with the front of the galleries. A large, handsome brass chandelier suspends from the middle of the centre. The outside of the church is adorned with Doric pilasters continued round the building, and a parapet-wall extends around the north and south side of the house. Between the pilasters is a double row of arched windows on the west and east side, the upper less in height than the lower. The steeple is 168 feet high, and is acknowledged the handsomest in America, and probably is not exceeded by any in London for the lightness of its architecture and the chasteness of its ornamentation.

---

[2] This gilt ball at the top of the steeple is of black cypress covered with copper, and was not hurt when it fell to the ground during a cyclone in 1885, although it made a spherical depression in the flagstones of the pavement.

ST. MICHAEL'S CHURCH, CHARLESTON, SOUTH CAROLINA
Sidewalk passing under porch.

· Detail at ·A·

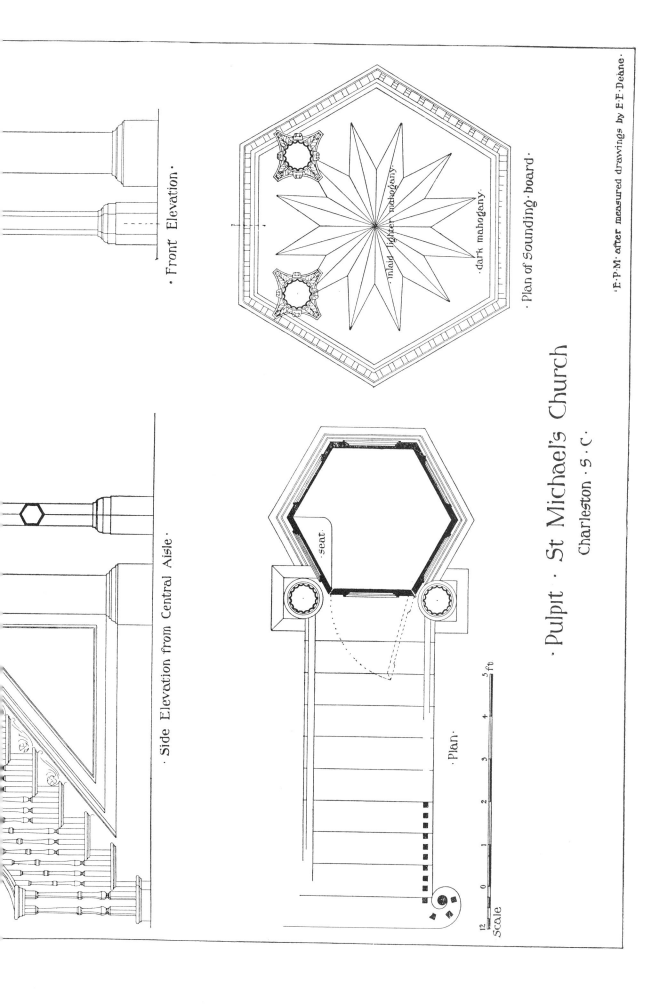

· Front Elevation ·

· Plan of Sounding · board ·

inlaid lighter mahogany.

dark mahogany.

· Side Elevation from Central Aisle ·

seat.

· Plan ·

Scale

5 ft

· Pulpit · St Michael's Church

Charleston · S · C ·

· E · P · M · after measured drawings by E · F · Deane ·

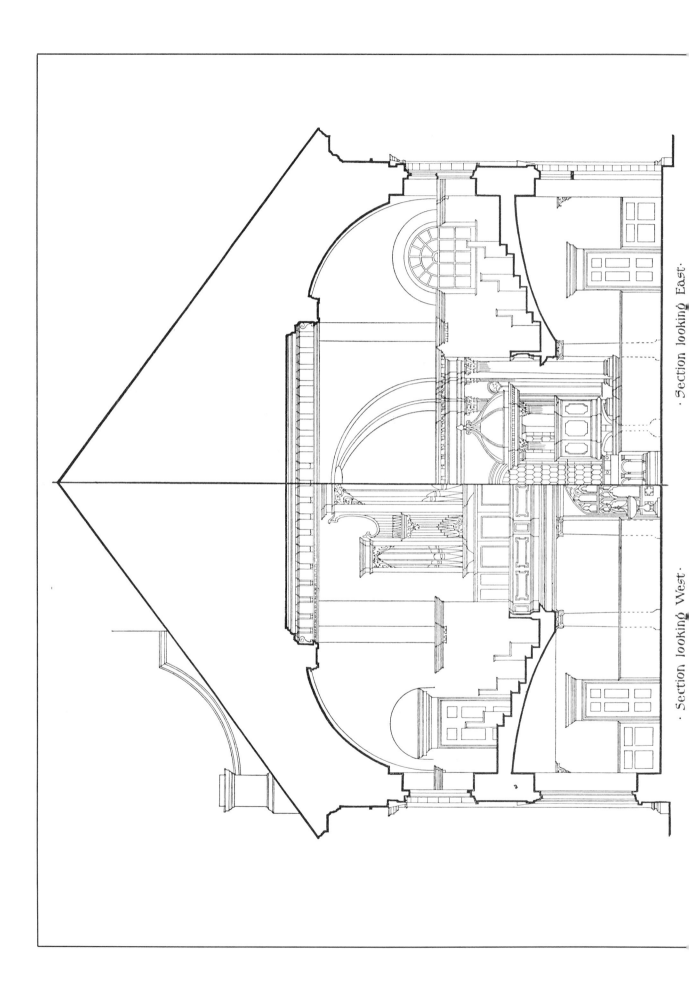

· Section looking East ·

· Section looking West ·

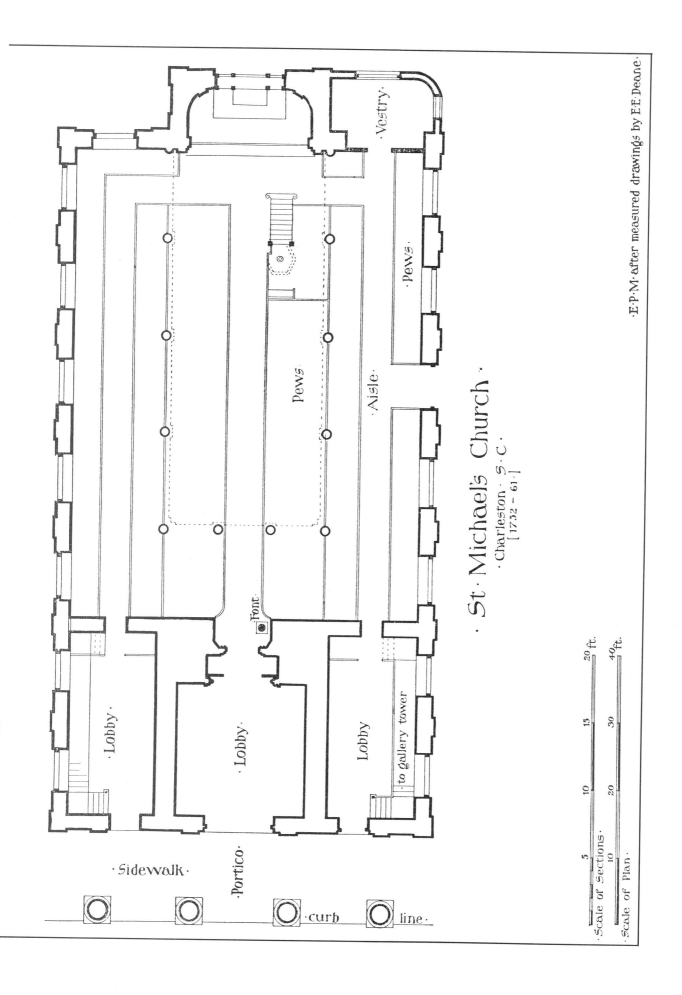

· St · Michael's Church ·
· Charleston · S · C ·
[1732 – 61 ·]

· Sidewalk ·

· Portico ·

· curb · line ·

Lobby ·

· Lobby ·

Lobby

· to gallery tower

Font ·

Pews

· Aisle ·

Pews ·

· Vestry ·

·E·P·M· after measured drawings by F.F. Deane.

· Scale of Sections ·
5   10   15   20 ft.

· Scale of Plan ·
10   20   30   40 ft.

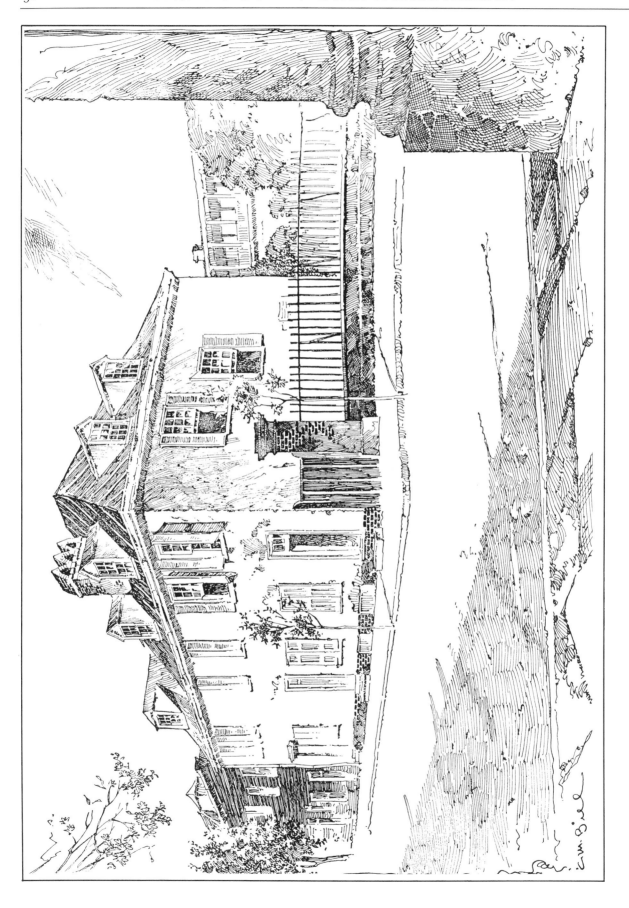

VIEW FROM ST. MICHAEL'S PORCH, CHARLESTON, SOUTH CAROLINA

Gateway

ST. MICHAEL'S CHURCHYARD, CHARLESTON, SOUTH CAROLINA

Interior
ST. MICHAEL'S CHURCH, CHARLESTON, SOUTH CAROLINA

Interior
ST. MICHAEL'S CHURCH, CHARLESTON, SOUTH CAROLINA

It is composed of a tower and spire. The tower is square from the ground and rises to a considerable height. The principal decoration of the lower part is a beautiful portico, with four Doric columns supporting an angular pediment, with modillion cornice. Over this rise two rustic courses; in the lower are small round sashed windows on the north and south sides, and in the second course are small square windows on each side. From this course the steeple rises octagonal, having windows with Venetian blinds on each face, with Ionic pilasters supporting arches whose cornice upholds a balustrade. Within this course is the belfry, in which is a ring of eight bells. The next course is likewise octagonal, but somewhat smaller than the lower, rising from within the balustrade. It has lofty sashed windows alternately on each face, with pilasters and a cornice. Here is the clock with dial-plate on the cardinal side. Upon this course rises, on a smaller octagonal base, a range of Corinthian pillars with a balustrade connecting them; the centres of the arches being ornamented with sculptured heads in relief. From hence is a beautiful and extensive prospect over town and harbor, and neighboring country and ocean. The body of the steeple is carried up octagonal within the pillars, on whose entablature a fluted spire rises. This is terminated by a globe 3 feet 6½ inches in diameter, supporting a vane 7 feet 6 inches long. The height of the steeple makes it the principal landmark for pilots.

"The building is said to have cost $32,775.87. This sum is apparently small, but we must take into consideration that everything since that time has advanced double or treble in price. Bricks were then bought for $3 per thousand, now [1819] they are $15. Lime was then six cents, now it is twenty cents per bushel, and everything else in proportion."

The bells[3] and clock were not imported until 1764.

<hr>

[3] "During the late Civil War the citizens of Charleston were desirous of protecting the bells from danger, and, as the steeple of St. Michael's was made the target for the cannon of the besiegers, the bells were taken down and sent to Columbia for safe keeping. When Sheridan's Army took Columbia the shed in the yard of the State-House, in which the bells had been placed, and which also contained the marble friezes and other sculptures intended for the decoration of the Capitol, were broken in and the sculptures and bells were smashed into fragments, and the sheds were then set on fire. At the conclusion of the war the pieces of the bells were carefully gathered together, boxed, and shipped to the commercial house of Frazier, Trenholm & Co., of Liverpool, together with extracts from the records of St. Michael's, showing where the bells were cast, and the proportions of the metals forming their component parts. Upon inquiry, it was found that there was still in existence in England the firm of bell-founders, unchanged in name, and consisting of the descendants of the proprietors at the time the bells were made. The records of this firm contained descriptions of the bells, and the proportions there given were found to correspond with those furnished from Charleston. The bells were made anew, therefore, of the same metal, and for the fifth time they were carried across the Atlantic, and arrived safely at Charleston. Their return was made the occasion of great rejoicing in the city."—*Washington Post, c1900.*

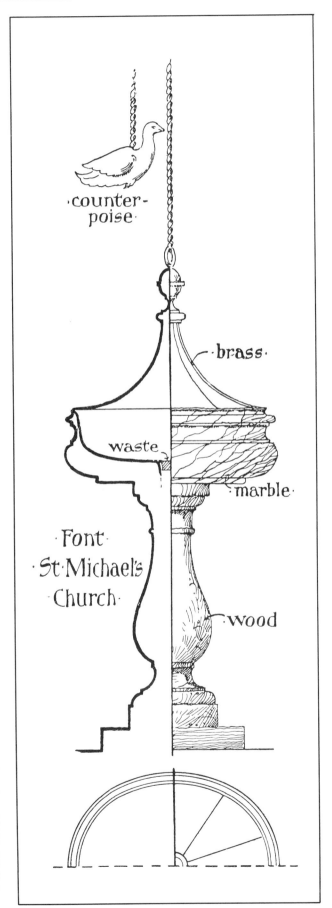

The bells cost in England £584 14 shillings, and the clock, which runs 30 hours, cost £194. The organ was imported in 1768, and cost £528. It was built by Mr. Schnetzler, and was greatly admired in London for its elegance of construction and brilliancy of tone.

St. Philip's Church has been called the Westminster Abbey of South Carolina because of the distinguished dead who lie about it. Perhaps no other churchyard in America contains the remains of so many men who have been illustrious in the history of the Church and the State, among whom may be mentioned Robert Daniel, a Landgrave (the only American title ever conferred by Great Britain) and a Governor of South Carolina, who was buried near the rising walls in 1718. Near him is John Logan, Speaker of the Commons; not far away is William Rhett, hero in the defense against the invasion of the French and Spanish in 1706, and of the expedition later against the pirates. Thomas Hepworth, Chief Justice, was buried there in 1728. "Good" Governor Robert Johnson — Governor both under the Proprietary and Royal Governments — was interred near the chancel in the churchyard. Four Chief Justices are laid here, of whom two were Peter Leigh and Charles Pinckney. Among the heroes of the Revolution who lie around the church are Christopher Gadsden and his right-hand man William Johnson. Rawlans Loundes, who was Governor in 1778, requested that the epitaph upon his tombstone should be "The opponent of the adoption of the Constitution of the United States." Edward Rutledge, signer of the Declaration of Independence, Col. Isaac Motte, second in command at the Battle of Fort Moultrie, also lie in St. Philip's churchyard. Thomas Pinckney, Major in the Continental Army, Major-General in the War of 1812, Minister to England and Spain, and Governor of the state, is also sleeping there. So is Rebecca Motte, the celebrated Revolutionary heroine, and many other notables of the same period. John C. Calhoun, the great nullifier, sleeps within the shadow of the old church, and near him are the remains of three other leaders in the great struggle of which he was the leader.

Edward McCrady, speaking on this subject, says: "Of the dignitaries of the Church in the line of the Episcopate there lie around her [St. Philip's] hallowed walls, two Commissaries of the Bishop of London, three Bishops of the American Church, and seven ministers who have served at her altar. Of chief magistrates, two Colonial and three State Governors are buried within her sacred precincts. Six Colonial Chief Justices worshipped in her sanctuary. Two Presidents of the Continental Congress and two signers of the Declaration of Independence were reared in the Church, one of the signers resting near her walls. Am-

bassadors and Ministers have gone from her to foreign lands, and members of Congress have been again and again chosen from her members. Soldiers of all the wars in which South Carolina, Province and State, has engaged lie within her gates. And there are also to be found the graves of men of science. It is believed that she has never been without a representation in the Senate or House of Representatives of the State Legislature. All the young men of the church went into the service of the Confederate States during the late war. And in the vestibule there is a memorial to those who gave their lives to their country."

The first edifice called by the name of St. Philip's was built on the site where St. Michael's now stands in 1681–2.[4] It was the first Church of England in South Carolina, and contemporary with "Old Ship" Church, Hingham, Massachusetts, and a few years later than Christ Church, Williamsburg, Virginia, which was built in 1678.

Unfortunately little is known concerning this early structure, beyond the fact that it was of black cypress, on a brick foundation, and that it was described in a letter of the period as "large and stately, surrounded by a neat white palisade fence." By 1723 the congregation had quite outgrown this simple church — "large and spacious" though it may have been — and was removed to the present site of St. Philip's on Church street, where a superb brick edifice was erected under an ordinance passed as early as 1710.

This second St. Philip's, which was opened for divine service on Easter Sunday, 1723, is the one of which Charlestonians of today still talk with affection and pride, and the history of which is closely identified with the pre-Revolutionary development of the state. The second St. Philip's was burned in 1835, the shingled roof of the tower having caught fire from the sparks of a neighboring conflagration. This particular bit of roofing was the vulnerable spot of the church, and caught fire once before in a similar manner from sparks from the Huguenot church on the next corner, and would have been destroyed then but for the resolute behavior of a negro slave who, seeing the danger, climbed up the spire and out on the roof, from which he ripped the burning shingles: for this heroic deed he received his freedom.[5]

The Charleston *Courier* of Feb. 16, 1835, has the following account of the burning of St. Philip's: —

"The most striking feature of this calamity is the destruction of St. Philip's Church, commonly known

---

[4] This date is given by Dr. Dalcho in his *Church History of South Carolina*. Edward McCrady, the eminent historian, thinks the date incorrectly given, though his research cause him to believe that it was erected prior to 1690.

[5] This deed is celebrated in a poem called "The Slave who saved St. Michael's," the author having credited the heroic deed to the wrong church.

ST. PHILIP'S CHURCH — 1835–1839 — CHARLESTON, SOUTH CAROLINA

as the "Old Church." The venerable structure, which has for more than a century (having been built in 1723) towered among us in all the solemnity and noble proportions of antique architecture, constituting a hallowed link between the past and the present, with its monumental memorials of the beloved and honored dead, and its splendid new organ (which cost $4,500) is now a smoking ruin. Although widely separated from the burning houses by the burial ground, the upper part of the steeple, the only portion of it externally composed of wood, took fire from the sparks which fell upon it in great quantities. It is much to be regretted that preventive measures had not been taken in season to save the noble and consecrated edifice. The flames, slowly descending, wreathed the steeple, constituting a magnificent spectacle, and forming literally a pillar of fire, finally enwrapping the whole body of the church in its enlarged volume. The burning of the body of the church was the closing scene of the catastrophy. In 1796 it was preserved by a negro man who ascended it, and was rewarded with his freedom for his perilous exertions; and again in 1810 it narrowly escaped the destructive fires of that year which commenced in the house adjoining the churchyard to the north.

"We have been informed that the only monument of the interior of the church which was not destroyed is one that, with accidental appropriateness, bears the figure of Grief."

Old St. Philip's, as the second church of the name is sometimes called to this day, was a more imposing structure than the one which bears the name today, and would have been, had it been spared, a notable example of the Colonial churches of America. Dr. Dalcho, in his oft-quoted *Church History of South Carolina,* gives the following verbose description of it: —

"St. Philip's Church stands on the east side of Church Street, a few poles north of Queen Street. It is built of brick and rough-cast. The nave is 74 feet long; the vestibule, or, more properly, the belfry, 37; the portico 12 feet and 22½ feet wide. The church is 62 feet wide. The roof is arched, except over the galleries; two rows of Tuscan pillars support five arches on each side, and the galleries. The pillars are ornamented on the inside with fluted Corinthian pilasters, whose capitals are as high as the cherubim, in relief, over the centre of each arch, supporting their proper cornice. Over the centre arch on the south side are some figures in heraldic form, representing the infant colony imploring protection of the King. The church was nearly finished when the King purchased the colony from the Lords Proprietors. This circumstance probably suggested the idea. Beneath the figures is this inscription: *Propius*

res aspice nostras. This has been adopted as the motto of the seal of St. Philip's Church. Over the middle arch on the north side is this inscription: *Deus mihi sol,* with armorial bearings, or the representation of some stately edifice.

"Each pillar is now ornamented with a piece of monumental sculpture, some of them with bas-relief figures finely executed by some of the first artists in England. These add greatly to the solemnity and beauty of the edifice. There is no chancel; the communion-table stands within the body of the church. The east end is a panelled wainscot ornamented with Corinthian pilasters, supporting the cornice of a fanlight. Between the pilasters are the usual tables of the Decalogue, the Lord's Prayer and the Apostles' Creed. The organ was imported from England, and had been used at the coronation of George II. The galleries were added subsequently to the building of the church. There are 88 pews on the ground floor and 60 in the galleries. Several of the pews were built by individuals at different times with the consent of the vestry. . . . The front of the church is adorned with a portico composed of four Tuscan columns supporting a double pediment. The two side-doors which open into the belfry are ornamented with round columns of the same order, which support angular pediments that project 12 feet; these give to the whole building the form of a cross, and add greatly to its beauty. This, however, is greatly obscured by the intervention of the wall of the graveyard. Pilasters of the same order with the columns are continued around the body of the church, and a parapet extends around the roof. Between each of the pillars is one lofty slashed window. Over the double pediment was originally a gallery with banisters which has since been removed as a security against fire. From this the steeple rises octagonal; in the first course are circular slashed windows on the cardinal side; and windows with Venetian blinds in each face of the second course, ornamented with Ionic pilasters, whose entablature supports a gallery. Within this course are two bells. An octagonal tower rises from within the gallery, having slashed windows on every other face and dial-plates of the clock on the cardinal side. Above is a dome upon which stands a quadrangular lantern. A vane in the form of a clock terminates the whole. Its height is probably 80 feet.

"St. Philip's Church has always been greatly admired. Its heavy structure, lofty arches and massive pillars, adorned with elegant sepulchral monuments, cast over the mind a feeling of solemnity highly favorable to religious impressions. The celebrated Edmund Burke, speaking of the church, said: 'It is spacious, and executed in very handsome taste, exceeding everything of that kind which we have in America,' and the

ST. MICHAEL'S, CHARLESTON, SOUTH CAROLINA

ST. PHILIP'S, CHARLESTON, SOUTH CAROLINA

Interior
ST. PHILIP'S CHURCH — 1836–1839 — CHARLESTON, SOUTH CAROLINA

biographer of Whitefield calls it a grand church, resembling one of the new churches of England in London."

No sooner was the second St. Philip's burned than a third was planned, the architect being Mr. J. Hyde, and its cornerstone was laid Nov. 12, 1835. It was built of brick, on the same foundation. For awhile the congregation would entertain no thought but to reproduce, as far as possible, the edifice they had lost, but within a year other counsel prevailed. Both churches, however, contained interior features peculiar to the Georgian period of church architecture, viz, galleries for congregation and choir, and a high pulpit adapted to them. Rev. John Johnson, D. D., who for the past thirty years has been rector of St. Philip's, gives the following description of the church as it stands today amid its countless graves.

"In regard to its external appearance the new St. Philip's differs not greatly from the old building. The same order of architecture was retained within, but with modifications that were improvements. Thus the massive square piers that supported the old church, that gave it some grandeur, and, faced with fluted pilasters bearing fine scriptural memorial tablets, some grace also, were not repeated because they darkened the interior, and interfered seriously with vision and hearing. The Doric order of the later (Roman) period gave rule, measure and proportion to the exterior of the new church, so that the columns, pilasters, and entablatures without the building represent very cor-

rectly, in all but the ornaments of capital and frieze, the order they illustrate. The interior of the sacred edifice is finished in the Corinthian order of architecture, and is the only specimen in the city of that order, with all the rich ornaments of the later, or Roman, period. These are executed, for the most part, in stucco, but the capitals of the columns are of carved wood. The roof and galleries are supported by eight fluted columns, four on each side, rising from pedestals of the same level as the rails of the pews to the height of twenty feet above the floors. There these columns, finished with their appropriate capitals, meet the line of the entablature, not extended in the usual way from column to column, but circumscribed above each column, so as to produce, with the overhanging cornice, the effect of a higher and larger capital, which, of course, it is not. This departure from the conventional design is something almost in the way of a *jeu d'esprit*. But it has its reason in the precedent of one of the finest churches in London by James Gibbs, architect, in 1721, and the express wish of the Charleston congregation to secure thereby the light and airy affect of the English prototype.

"At a meeting of the congregation of St. Philip's, June 27, 1836, it was resolved, 'that the heavy pillars of the interior of the church be dispensed with, and that in lieu thereof Corinthian columns, as far as possible after the style of St. Martin's-in-the-Fields, London, be adopted.' And again resolved, 'that the pillars of the plan presented be lowered, so as to reduce the

Interior
ST. PHILIP'S CHURCH — 1836–1839 — CHARLESTON, SOUTH CAROLINA

arches.' These arches were the motives of the whole scheme. Springing longitudinally from the square of cornice above each column at an altitude of about twenty-five feet and rising at their crown to a level of thirty-six feet above the floor, these fine arches on each side support the roof, and contribute no little to the beauty of the interior, lifting the eye above the columns and galleries to the topmost ceiling of the church, forty-two or forty-three feet above the floor. The crown of each arch is ornamented with a cherub's head and wings in stucco, while in the spaces of the spandrels between the shoulders of the arches the same material is used for the display of the acanthus ornamentation. The unbroken entablature is seen in the chancel where it passes from one pilaster to another, but is again broken by the head of the high stained-glass window. Above the cornice of the chancel the coved ceiling is ribbed and adorned with rosettes in stucco. On either side of the chancel the walls are enriched by tablets inscribed as usual."

Dr. Johnson gives the dimensions of the building in feet as follows: —

Extreme length of building, including porch 120
Extreme width of building, exclusive of south
   and north porches 62
Projection of porches 12
Height of walls on side 35
Height of ridge of roof 45
Height of steeple 200

INTERIOR DIMENSIONS

Extreme length of church 114
Depth of chancel 9
Width of chancel 24
Extreme width of church 56
Height of galleries (upper rail) 14
Extreme height of ceiling 42
Width of vestibule 20

The cost of the new St. Philip's, as reported to the congregation on the 15th of July, 1839, was $84,206.01. Later, however, a steeple and spire, surmounted by a plain gold cross, were added, after a design by Edward B. White, which must have raised the total cost to nearly $100,000. When the steeple was completed, early in the 1850s, a clock with a chime of bells was presented to it by Mr. Colin Campbell, of Beaufort. These were taken down at the beginning of the war and presented to the Confederate government to be cast into cannon.

During the war the steeples of St. Michael's and St. Philip's, being the most conspicuous objects in the city, served as targets for the Federal guns. Of the two thus subjected to fire St. Philip's suffered most, as ten or more shells entered her walls. The chancel was destroyed, the organ demolished, and the roof pierced in several places. The congregation continued to worship in the church, however, until Thanksgiving Day, 1863, and returned to it again as soon as the war was over.

· Chancel Rail · St · Michael's Church · Charleston · S · C

· Outside Gate · St · Philip's Church · Charleston · S · C ·
[· Possibly the Communion Rail · in · the · former · St · Philip's Church ·]

· Scale ·

· Scale ·

An Autumn Trip to
South Carolina

Text by
E. Eldon Deane
Originally published in 1902 as
Volume III of the Georgian Period

S! Philip's Ch: seen from S! Michael's

AN AUTUMN TRIP TO SOUTH CAROLINA

IT was the sense of profound, if temporary, relief from the noise and restless turmoil of cosmopolitan New York, that I metaphorically shook off its dust from my feet on a close and oppressive afternoon in late September of last year, and boarded the steamer for Charleston, South Carolina, a city so dimly pictured in my imagination from only too scanty descriptions of the earthquake days that I drew down the mental curtain and consigned myself to a couple of days' absolute rest, wondering the deep waters had not sense enough to rest too. After a seemingly endless and nauseating period of sensationalism in the daily press, unfolding the corruption and vice of the city under Crokerism and Tammany rule, it was a blessed privilege to flee, even temporarily, from this modern Sodom and Gomorrah. As the evening drew on, how bracing was the cool air and how welcome the silence brooding over the deep as we slipped down the Jersey shore, just far enough out to see the blinking lights of the various summer resorts, without their garishness or even the faint echo of their noisy crowds. Saturday passed refreshingly as we rounded the capes, with a good sea on, and Sunday morning opened sublimely, with expectancy on the faces of all, for the evening would see us at our destination. Nor were we disappointed, for about four o'clock we slipped between the breakwaters into the beautiful and expansive harbor and, passing the historic Fort Sumter, by half past five o'clock we were snugly moored alongside one of the old shaky piers, looking down into the faces of the little dusky crowd peering up at us from among the bales of cotton and promiscuous cargo on the wharves.

The approach to the city is disappointing, wanting in architectural interest, the buildings being low, the city itself lying on a peninsula as flat as an ironing board, between the two rivers, Cooper on the east and Ashley on the west. One looked for an interesting skyline and found none; only the two steeples of St. Philip's and St. Michael's broke the roofline and pierced the azure with their graceful spires. The only building on the waterline to attract notice is the new customhouse, with its stately proportions and colonnaded porticos. Before walking down the gangplank a new-made acquaintance remarked as he bade me adieu: "You won't be half a day in this dead town before you will wish yourself well out of it."

This is the general impression of businessmen passing through, or by, historic old Charleston. The interest to a stranger depends on the point of view taken. Charleston is only awakening from a long slumber, the natural sequence of a series of paralyzing circumstances. The wharves of this city will not always be so silent as they are today. With the resuscitation of the South her commerce is bound to revive, and, with her natural advantages, we shall see her roadsteads alive with shipping and the silence broken with the sirens of the transatlantic liners.

Looking at Charleston from the aesthetic and architectural point of view, the historic city teems with interest. Unique in its type of palatial residences, with amplitude of light, air and space, it is of the past that it speaks, and a past to be proud of. But, desirable as is a new era of prosperity, one quakes in contemplation of the changes that a modern affluence will bring in its wake. Once let in the entering wedge of Northern energy, capital and ideas, the steel structure and skyscraper, the flat-roofed abominations of the modern economic system, will quickly eliminate the sense of leisure and restfulness that pervades the city of today.

After leaving the steamer and after a shaky ride over the cobblestones, we were deposited at the Hotel Charleston, and, pending the late-houred supper, a twilight voyage of discovery was in order. This was Sunday evening, and the principal streets appeared to be given over to the colored population, who in summer attire, especially the young folks, promenaded with an importance and gaiety entirely their own. Otherwise the city seemed deserted, and the sense of

Entrances
HEYWARD ESTATE, MEETING STREET, CHARLESTON

strangeness became oppressive. As the darkness deepened, the artistic features of the old streets were intensified, revealing more of incidental worth than in the garishness of midday: high walls with ramped copings, tall gateposts and great heavy rustic oak and iron gates, over which creep lovely vines, and beyond which frown the dark spaces of the colonnaded galleries, with, may be, some little wicket in the rear opening on a tree-embowered lawn, all in deep shadow, while the old brick chimneys and Spanish-tiled roofs peep over the trees and are silhouetted against an amber sky. The sidewalk pavements are mostly of brick, set herringbone fashion, with a deep curbstone down to the cobblepaved streets. The gates are threefold, adjoining the front door, which opens upon the side gallery, generally a few feet raised up; first, the private, or domestic, gate; secondly, the carriage gates, and a narrower one adjoining for the servants, which used in slave days to be closed at nine o'clock in the evening, and no colored person could enter after that time without being detected. A curfew bell tolled at half past eight to call in the colored servants, and after nine o'clock a colored person was not to be seen on the streets. After treading the streets in and out, poking around church corners, astonished to find cemeteries creeping up to the very houses, and headstones almost peeping in at one's dining room window, it was with a sense of the general mouldiness of the city—an eerie feeling, arousing one's curiosity for the morrow's light—that I returned to the hotel. True to my friend's prophecy, I was not in the city twenty-four hours before, for some reasons, I might have wished myself out of it, for, of all the cities I have ever visited, never was there culinary capability so behind the times, never was one's patience so put to test over loss of time in replenishing the inner man. How in the world the visitors to the Exposition have been accommodated would be interesting to hear. But aside

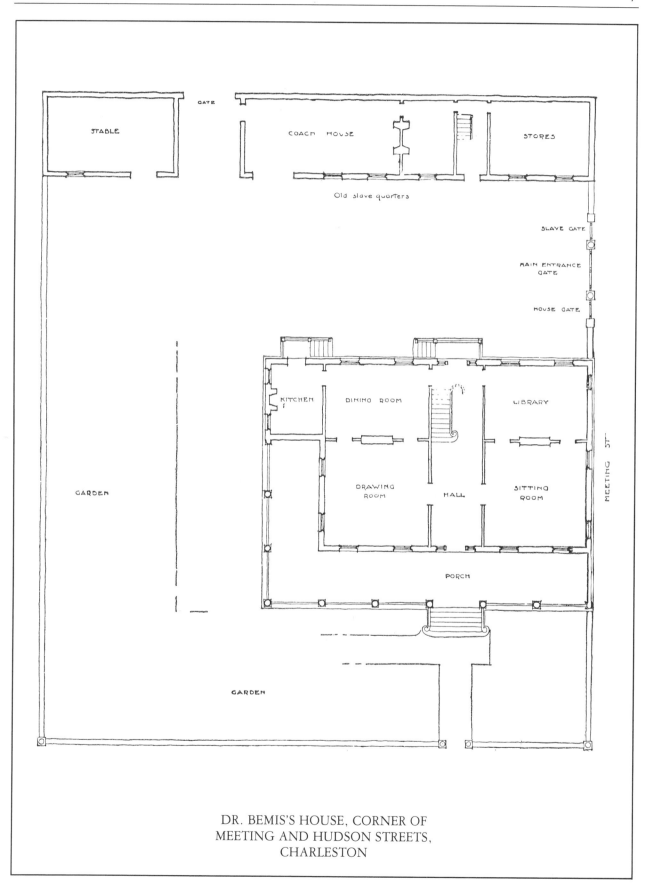

DR. BEMIS'S HOUSE, CORNER OF
MEETING AND HUDSON STREETS,
CHARLESTON

The "Joggling Board"

from this little blemish, the interest in the city grows. In plan practically another, but Old Colonial, New York, the names of the streets suggest British origin and dominion, and to this day are tenaciously preserved and cherished—King Street, Queen Street, Meeting Street, Church Street, etc. Laid out at right angles, the residence plots, or blocks, are very large, affording spacious gardens and court yards. Every residence used to be walled in with high walls and gates, ensuring privacy and seclusion, but now few of these are in anything like good preservation. As an old Charlestonian was pleased to put it to me, "The city was settled by the English and Huguenots, they intermarrying you have the American, who cannot be whipped." The city is essentially English in its houses and customs, its domestic life and its tastes. The earliest houses were of plainest description, simplest in plan, fronting on the street, the entrance opening into a hall dividing equally the rooms, right and left, and with basement kitchens; but as the colony progressed, and the retinue of colored help increased, a change of plan developed, and the typical house evolved, with its end to the street, its front opening on the garden, and with wide galleries, or verandas, overlooking the rear of its neighbor. The slave or servants' quarters generally were in a brick extension at the other end of the house, though exceptions there were, in which they were built away from the house, around the court yard.

In the city's palmy days intercourse with England was the rule, not the exception, and clothes, furniture, glass and silverware were all imported, as were also the wines—madeira and sherry. The madeira was always stored in the attic, for the benefit of a certain condition of temperature. In the city, at least, the servants were always well clothed, uniformed or in livery, and treated like children, as indeed they were.

The kitchens were now outside the house proper, and the meals were served from these outside kitchens by the colored help, through the medium of a pantry adjoining the dining room. Thus all odoriferous objections were eliminated from the family quarters. Strange it was to note that in no ancient house in its primitive condition did I observe any toilet or bathroom accessories. The valet or maid used to bring up the bathtub and then the water, put you in it, if you liked, rub you down, and carry all away again. Talk about sanitation—what could be sweeter and healthier than that? Now, what is it? An impoverished family keep one or perhaps two servants, or no servant, in a large old barrack of a house, with a forlorn and antediluvian system of kitchen and toilet-room accommodation. Think of the transition! What few draperies are left are moth-eaten and faded, carpets threadbare and the onetime garden a desolation and wilderness. But there are the galleries left—oh, those cool, shady retreats, with their wide sweeps, and which you can picture with their happy and lively occupants of the older days! Here you can live out the better half of the hot summer days; somewhere you are pretty sure of a shaded corner, swept by a cool breeze, and down on the lower gallery the sounds of a merry group of youngsters tell you of the good time they are having on the old "joggling-board." This was an article entirely new to me, and I was curious to know what the sensation of the thing was that could make such an odd piece of furniture so indispensable in every household. It was, I believe, first instituted for the little pickaninnies, and consists of a long, two-inch-thick pine board, say twenty-five feet long, supported on two framed end trestles or horses. These trestles are sometimes fitted on rockers. Well, calling one evening at the house of a friend, the lady asked if I would not prefer to sit out of doors in the cool, and archly proffered me the joggling-board. Assenting, I fear, with dubious air, the good lady, who represented a fair figure in avoirdupois, took the initiative and I followed, when with an alternating motion of up and down we were joggled to the center of the board and into such an embarassing proximity that only an explosion of laughter suited the occasion. Now you can picture, when a group of youngsters of susceptible age and both sexes, in the cool of the evening or moonlit night, plump themselves down on this stout but pliable plank what nonsense and hilarity they get out of it.

But for absolute fun commend me to the colored pickaninnies, and even their elders, the aunties and uncles, one or more thrumming on the "ole banjo," the others taking up the chorus of "My Ole Kentucky Home" in melodious song. No darky home appeared to be complete without the joggling-board, and some specimens which had seen ancient service were beauti-

THE BATTERY AND DE SAUSSURE HOUSE, CHARLESTON

fully put together, and even wear and tear seemed only to have rounded the edges more invitingly.

Days went apace, and what with tramping, sketching and measuring in a heat that sometimes was torrid, evening and its cool breezes from the Battery overlooking the harbor were very grateful. There was a reserve very perceptible in the attitude of the residents towards intrusion on their secluded homes, and it took time to overcome this. The tourist and Kodak fiend had in their overpresumptuous recklessness caused annoyance aforetime which was resented; but as soon as my real mission was made known every facility was offered and kindly courtesy extended on every hand. Still, it was regrettable that so much of my so little time had to be spent in awaiting permission. After spending a couple of weeks in the city, I made the visit to Georgetown and the Santee district, which occupied a week, and then returning spent another week in Charleston. The interval and change of scenery acted as a tonic and, returning, helped qualify my first impressions. Strange it is, but, ever and everywhere, it is just as you are departing you see more, and find out more, to regret the limit of your stay. What are three weeks in a large city, single-handed and three-quarters of your time being taken up with those necessary but provokingly objectionable adjuncts, the measuring tape and foot rule? With so much to tempt one to brushwork, it was hard to put the palette aside for the severer practical work of measuring.

Sunday was the Sunday of our forefathers, and in its decorous observance I was pleased to observe that the colored population appeared entirely devout. In this most English city, how I enjoyed the English service in the old churches of St. Michael and St. Philip. After nearly twenty years' absence from the old country, here was a rendering of the service on the old lines, awakening cherished memories of the past—the quaint old-time edifice, the sweet bells, the mellow tones of an organ built in 1767, that Handel himself might have played on, the high-decked pulpit and square high-backed pews, and the obsequious old sexton. Through the open side doors, through which a flood of sunshine poured and quaint white tombstones peeped, came the subdued sounds of city life, with the chirruping of the birds and the perfume of box and the evergreen shrubbery of the churchyard. It is easy to picture the same service of forty or a hundred and twenty years ago, with the Governor and his retinue occupying his pew near the pulpit, perhaps the Father of his Country standing erect beside him, the buzz of curiosity as they enter and leave the church, the rows of colored people who occupy benches around the sides and end of the building or in the galleries, the waiting carriages, the old beadle with gold-tipped cane escorting the dignitaries thereto, the handshaking at the doors, smiles, congratulations and all the social amenities of the time. The only discordant note of today is the harsh metallic grinding of the trolley-car as it whizzes by or turns the corner into Broad Street.

If you wish to obtain a comprehensive view of the city, a climb up the tower and steeple of either church

is well rewarded, for, in the absence of any natural altitudes, your vision is limited to the perspectives of the streets and your neighbors' residences on all sides of you. From the church steeple you look northward away over the city to its very limits, the rivers Ashley and Cooper stretching on either side, exactly as do the North and East rivers about Manhattan—and then down over the roofs and into the shady and spacious gardens, squares and parks. Southward you have the magnificent harbor and islands. From this altitude you realize what a magnificent city it must have been in its palmy days: truly patrician in its character and, as I first beheld it at sunset, a little world of loveliness in itself.

Of the two church towers and spires that of St. Philip's is the most graceful, while that of St. Michael's suggests stateliness. Built of brick and rough-cast, its cream-white walls and surfaces, as it pierces the clearest of blue skies, are rather dazzling but beautiful in effect; and again, as I saw it on a moonlight night, in the stillness and repose of the city, the memory of its vicissitudes set me dreaming, to be aroused suddenly by the sound of the melodious and historic bells, as they chimed the quarters, followed by the tolling of the hour. There is a fascination about this church and its steeple, placed as it is at the corner, or junction of two principal streets, dominating every building and feature in its vicinity, that charms and arrests your interest whenever you pass it. Were I asked what features charmed me most in Charleston, my reply would be: "St. Michael's Church and the Miles Brewton House," better known as the Bull-Pringle House. And as I was privileged to sit in the old Pringle pew on Sunday morning the harmony of the relationship between the two was not lost in my musings.

After a pretty close study of the older residences here, the absence of the more delicate and refined ornaments of the Colonial type, to be found in the more northern states, becomes evident, and more or less disappointing, with one exception, and that is the Brewton House, which, while simple and plain in its plan, sturdy in the construction and stately in effect, is beautiful as a whole, the drawing room and reception rooms especially so. It were well worth the while that the whole house should be measured carefully, and not a mere room or two, which was all I could give the time to, and, further, it being furnished and occupied, the concession made by the lady of the house was sufficiently appreciated without putting her to more trouble and disarrangement. The old garden, now very much circumscribed in its area, was in the early days a vision of loveliness, and to this day the old-time tulips, jonquils, daffodils, peonies, send up their perennial bevy of bloom and color, while ancient wistarias bend the branches of stout trees with their weight of superabundant leafage and tassels of turquoise blue. During the earthquake this sturdy old house suffered the least of all, only one wall panel

SOUTH CAROLINA SOCIETY'S BUILDING

Drawing Room
BULL-PRINGLE (MILES BREWTON) HOUSE, CHARLESTON, SOUTH CAROLINA

BULL-PRINGLE (MILES BREWTON) HOUSE—1765—LOWER KING STREET.
CHARLESTON, SOUTH CAROLINA

BULL-PRINGLE (MILES BREWTON) HOUSE — 1765 — LOWER KING STREET, CHARLESTON, SOUTH CAROLINA

Drawing Room

BULL-PRINGLE (MILES BREWTON) HOUSE, CHARLESTON, SOUTH CAROLINA

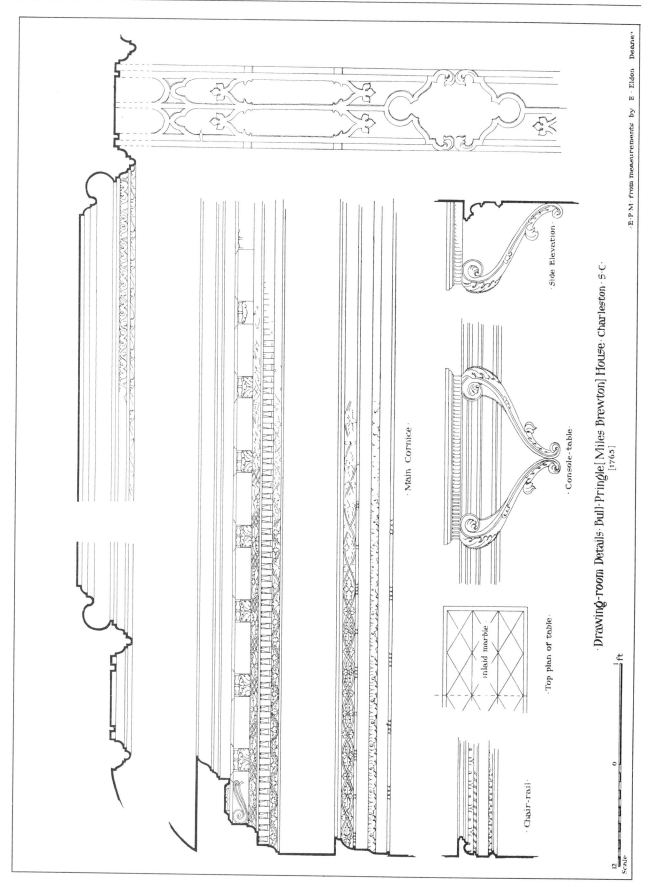

· Main Cornice ·

· Side Elevation ·

· Console · table ·

inlaid marble

· Top plan of table ·

· Chair · rail ·

· Drawing · room Details · Bull · Pringle [Miles Brewton] House · Charleston · S·C ·

[1765]

· E·P·M· from measurements by E· Eldon Deane ·

Scale

12 · · · · 0 · · · · 1 ft

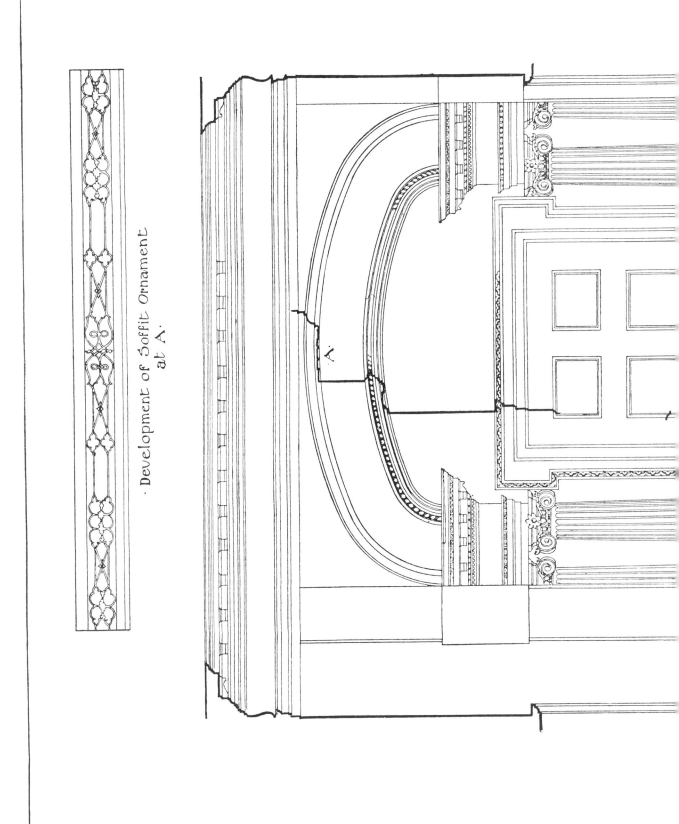

· Development of Soffit Ornament
at A.

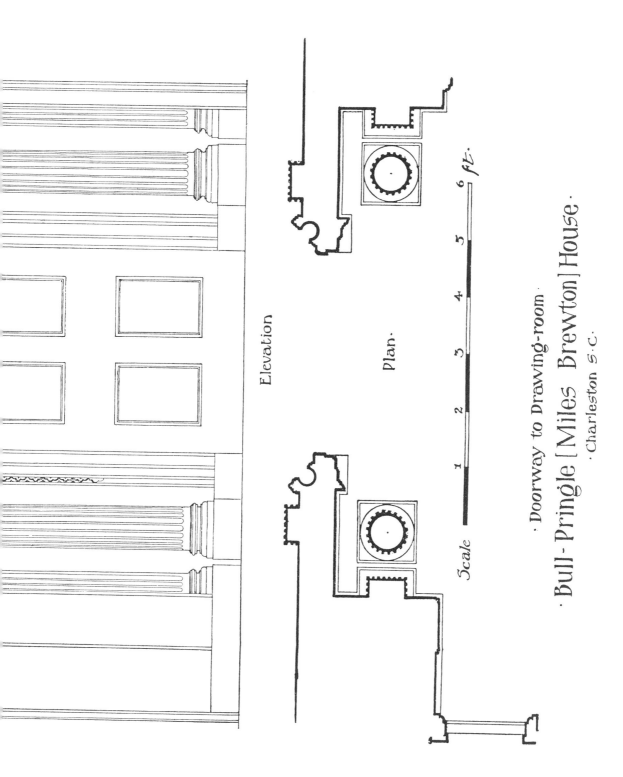

Elevation

Plan.

Scale

1 2 3 4 5 6 ft.

· Doorway to Drawing-room ·

· Bull-Pringle [Miles Brewton] House ·

· Charleston S·C·

· C·M·D· from measurements by E·E·Deane ·

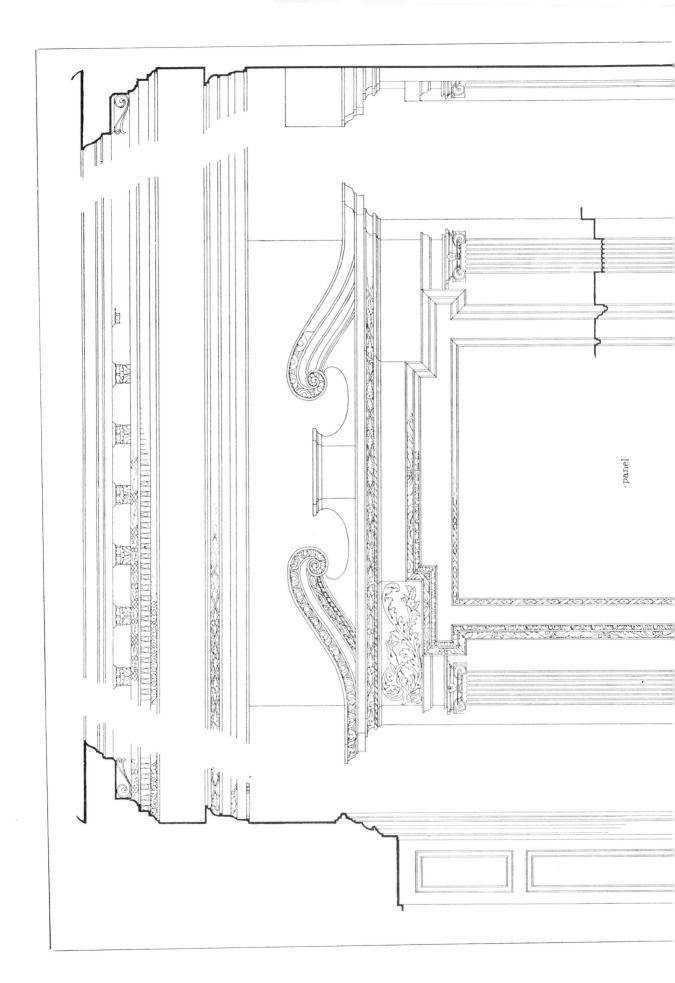

·panel·

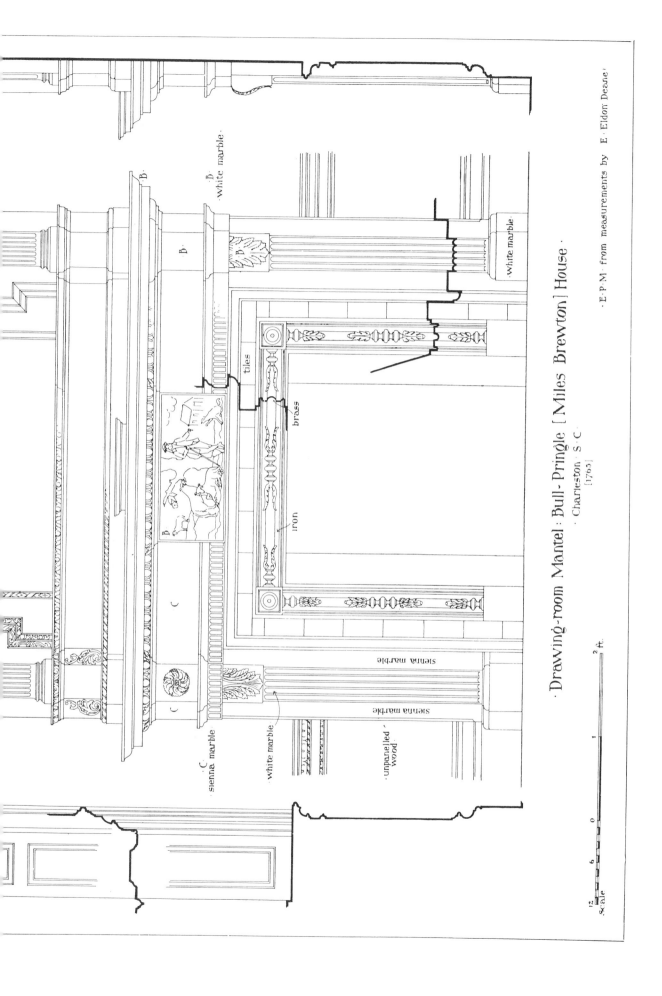

· Drawing-room Mantel : Bull - Pringle [Miles Brewton] House ·

· Charleston · S · C ·

[1765]

· E·P·M· from measurements by E · Eldon Deane ·

Scale

B.

B.
white marble.

B.

B.

white marble.

tiles

brass

iron

sienna marble

sienna marble

C.

C.

sienna marble.

white marble

unpanelled wood.

· Detail at ·A·

Drawing-room: Bull Pringle [Miles
[1765]

0   3   6   9   12 ins.
· Scale of detail ·
0   1   2   3   4   5 ft.
· scale of Elevation ·

Brewton] House · Charleston · S · C ·

· E · P · Morrill from measurements by E · Eldon Deane ·

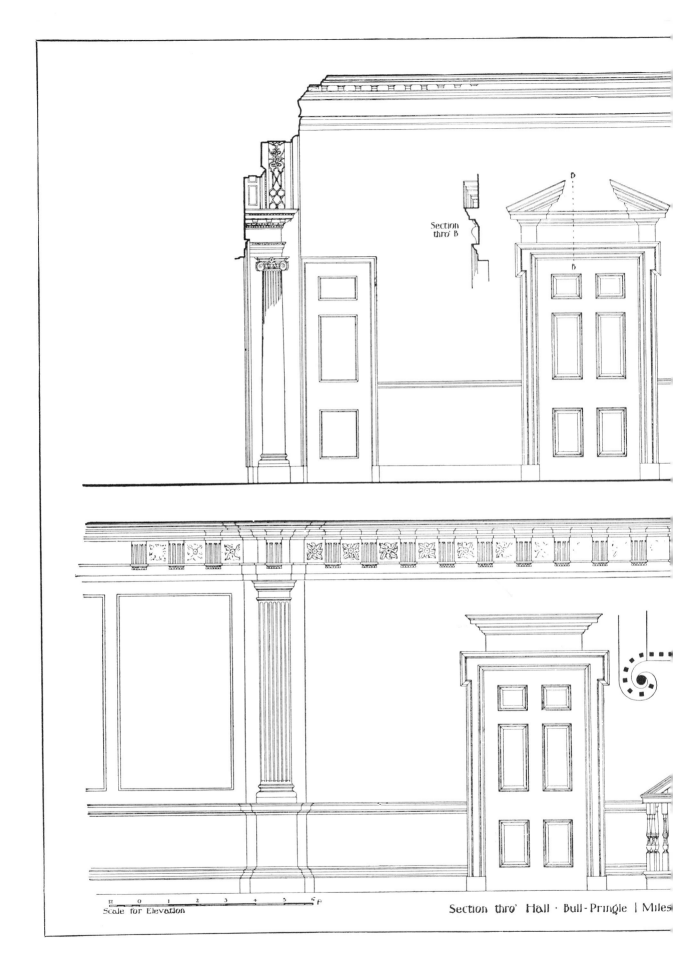

Section
thro' B

Scale for Elevation

Section thro' Hall · Bull-Pringle | Miles

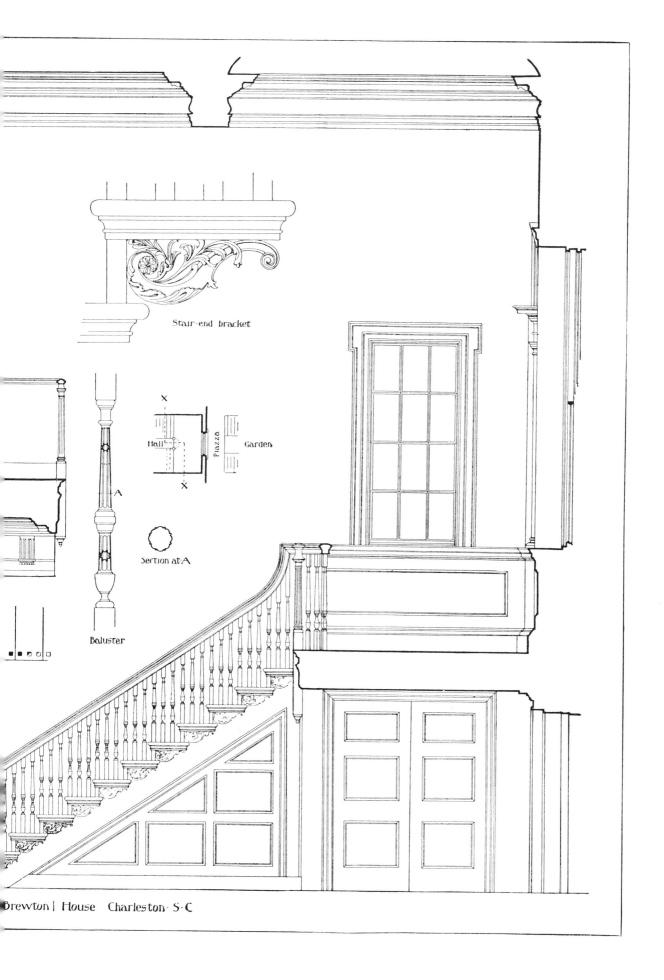

Stair-end bracket

X

Hall　Piazza　Garden

X

A

Section at A

Baluster

Brewton House　Charleston·S·C

·Section thro' Staircase on line· X·X·

·Bull·Pringle [Miles Brewton] House·

·Charleston·S·C·

·Scale· 12   0   1   2   3 ft.

·E·P·M· from measurements by ·E·E·Deane·

Interior
ST. MICHAEL'S CHURCH, CHARLESTON, SOUTH CAROLINA

being cracked, thanks to English-built walls of two feet six inches thickness, while those more recently built on the Battery or promenade suffered most, due to their sites being all "made ground," in fact what originally was swamp.

Romance suffuses this old house with an interest far in excess of its neighbor's. As you walk the garden-paths it can be pointed out where the ruthless Northerners, after churning up the priceless old china—which had been previously packed by loving and anxious fingers, for safe hiding—with the butts of their rifles, then strewed it. Though occupied during the War of the Revolution by Lord Rawdon and his staff as his headquarters, little damage was done, compared to the ruffianly treatment of the Union soldiers; but, after all, considering the crises it has passed through, the house is wonderfully well preserved.

Recalling the story of the occupation of the Brewton House by the British officers and their courteous treatment by Mrs. Rebecca Motte and her daughter—on the day after capitulation she entertained both British and American officers at the same table and won

golden opinions from all—the old prayer-book and Bible, with her name inscribed, was bought at a book-stall in London by one of these same officers and returned by him to Mrs. Motte. The old Bible is still, so I hear, read in the quaint little Church of St. James, Santee.

Judge Heyward's house on Church Street has its plan and several features in common with the Brewton House, but it is not of so large proportion, nor are its enrichments so profuse; but there is a sense of comfort, as well as stateliness, in the drawing room measured. The Horrey House, corner of Tradd and Meeting streets, is remarkable for its double-decked portico, or veranda, over the sidewalk, supported on stone columns of Tuscan and Ionic orders, while within the features are plain and substantial, but with meager ornament, and what there is is rather coarse.

The Elliot House—now used as a pumping-station (the water supply is from an artesian well two thousand feet deep, and is pumped into a little reservoir in the yard; the water is quite hot when first pumped up but is allowed to cool before its distribution)—has

It should be remembered that here were the summer houses of the rich planters who found it unwholesome and impossible to live out the summer on their plantations. I was told that really their plantation-houses were better and more solidly built than their city houses, which were intended, after all, only for summer use, and under these circumstances space, light and air were their chief requisites.

The Thomas Ball House uptown, on the East Battery, is a type quite common; that is, a whole house built only one room deep, with a central hall, with front and rear balconies, or verandas. Here it may incidentally be remarked that there are several of these extensive old barracks which could be soon converted into more comfortable and civilized houses, and are to be rented for a merely nominal figure. There was one fine old place, with its house-servants and carriage-house and front and rear court yards, rented for only $25 per month, but—well, that is down in Charleston!

One of the old-time features of the city is the market, of such a length as to suggest walking over Brooklyn Bridge, in this respect, that you wonder when it is coming to an end. Its terminal, or entrance, is in the form of a two-storied Greek temple, the upper story being used as offices and reached by a double flight of stairs, the entrance to the market being through a wide arch under these. Seen at its best—on market day, or night—it presents a weird aspect. About fifty feet wide, it runs in four sections, necessitated by four intersecting streets, and in total must reach about eight hundred feet. A broad central flagged walk is flanked on either side by stalls, in appearance like

little peculiar interest beyond the ample reception hall, from which a central flight of stairs conducted to an upper hall, with a large well and gallery on all sides; but this has been cut away to make room for the pumping-engines. The rooms are very spacious and the mantels and door finish and cornices of the general type of the period, *i. e.*, the beginning of the nineteenth century.

There are many old houses which have historic interest and more or less romance, but are deficient in detail worth carrying away. What one notices in traversing the length of the city—which is best done by a loop-line of the trolley-system—is the change from the earliest-planned, or English, type of house downtown, fronting on the street, and the gradual development to the typical Charleston house as built before the war.

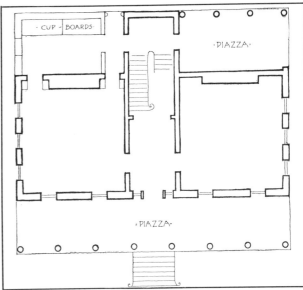

THOMAS BALL HOUSE, CHARLESTON,
SOUTH CAROLINA

CHARLESTON MARKET — 1841 — CHARLESTON

those of a stable, and the unbroken monotony is remarkable. The roof is a simple king-post affair, open, and adds to the endless perspective. But the strangest feature to Northern eyes is the presence of those natural scavengers, the buzzards, who make their appearance only during market hours, and at its close take their flight to their own eyries. To see them in their descent from the roof to the cobblestones after some bit of carrion is very attractive; they come down with such a clumsy swoop you expect to see them tumble and break their necks; but no, with a sweeping curve close to the ground they alight like thistledown and run with such sidelong gait and so swiftly that you cannot restrain a laugh.

In some of the later houses, as, for instance, the Russell, the Witte and others, a unique feature is the staircase, which is built in a circular or oval plan, and self-supporting from the ground it rests upon to the landing on the next floor, independent of the walls, which it does not touch, saving a good deal of space and generally placed so as to afford a roomy rear hall.

Some pleasant side-trips are to be made from Charleston, by boat or trolley, as, for instance, to the Lowndes, or Waggoner, homestead on the Ashley River, used during the Exposition as the Woman's Building; also the Turnbull and Lawton estates, the former metamorphosed by municipal authorities for park purposes, and the latter included in the site for the Naval Station, the house, I believe, being originally in the possession of the Izard family. Other excursions by train and yet within reach of an hour or two's journey, are Goosecreek Church and Mulberry Castle, on the Cooper River, and Pompion Hill Church and Drayton Hall, on the Ashley River. The latter house I regretted my inability to see, as the place was closed up and the family away.

To sum up my impressions of Charleston: I found it a proud old city, with every evidence of wealth and luxury in its past, but there is scarcely an estate upon which the inscription "Ichabod" could not be appropriately placed on its gateposts. Without the help, the spacious gardens are but poorly kept up, and reflect the all-pervading decay. As you behold all these big mansions, and after talking with their owners, you are manifestly impressed with the distinction of having a grandfather who helped to make history, but reflect

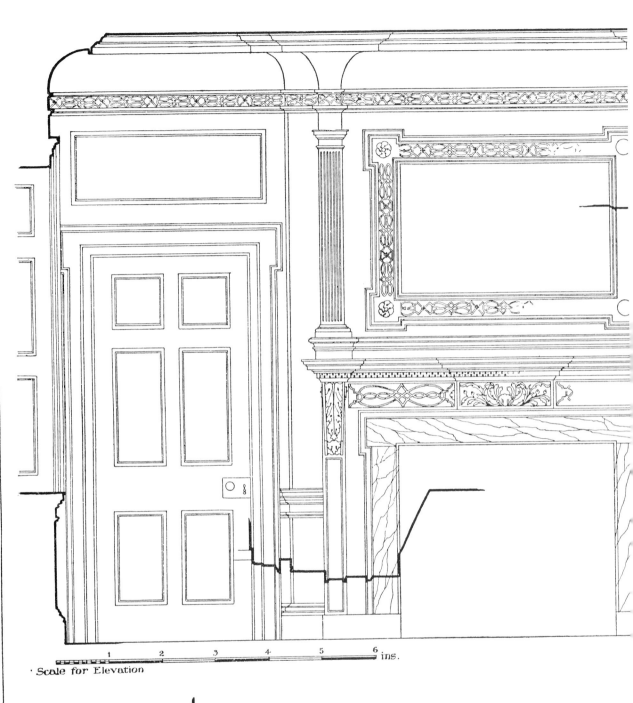

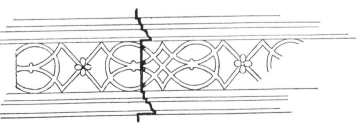

Scale for Elevation

1 2 3 4 5 6 ins.

Drawing-room Wall
Judge Heyward's

Detail of fretwork on Chimney-breast

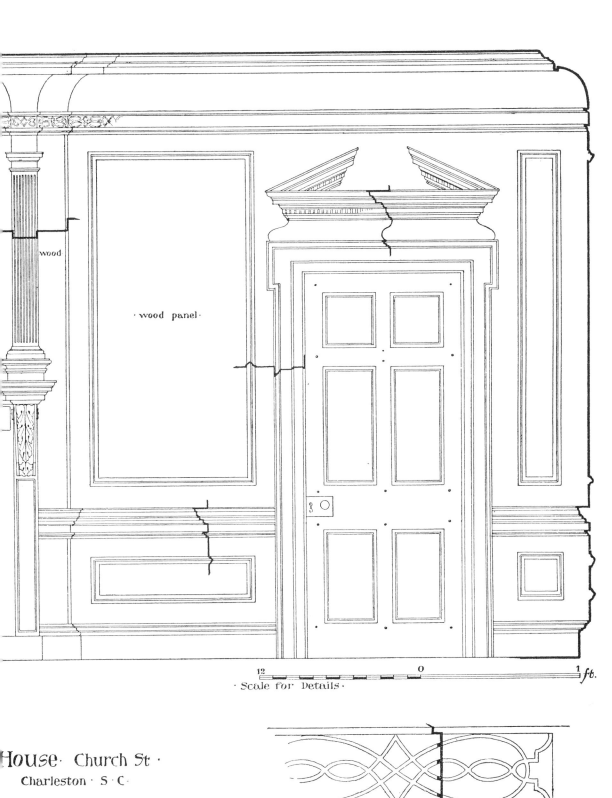

· wood ·

· wood panel ·

12   0   1 ft.

· Scale for Details ·

House · Church St ·

Charleston · S · C ·

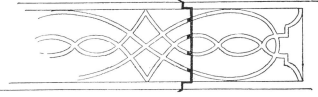

· Detail of fretwork below mantel

· E · P · M · after measured sketches by E · Eldon Deane ·

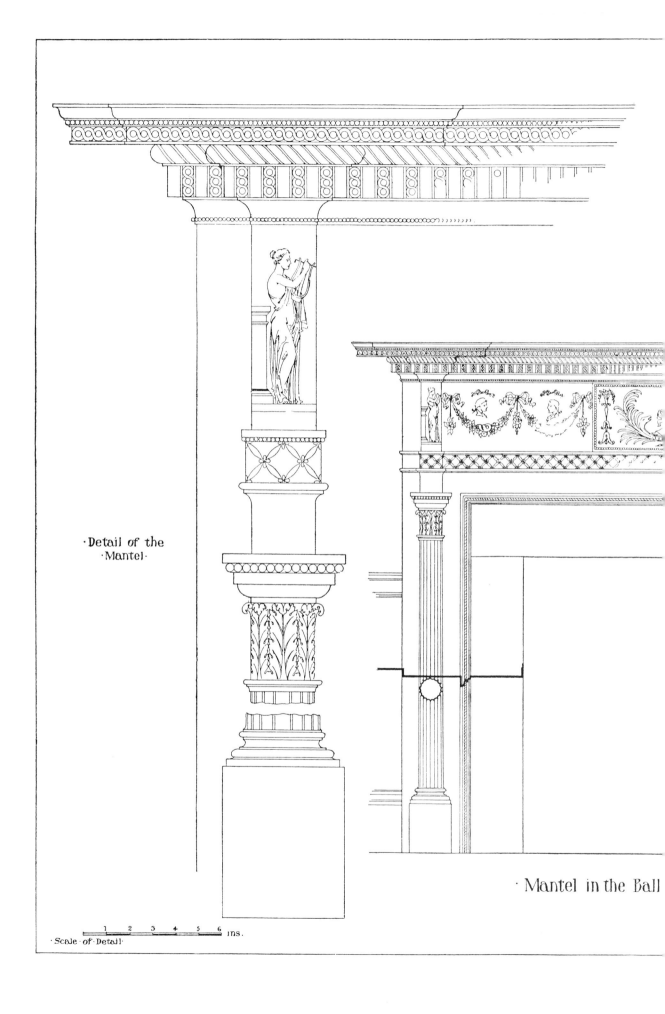

·Detail of the
·Mantel·

·Scale·of·Detail·

1 2 3 4 5 6 ins.

· Mantel in the Ball

Plan of Shelf ·

House · Carolina St · ·

·Charleston · S · C ·

12   9   6   3   0   1   2 ft.

· Scale of Elevation ·

E · P · M · after measured drawings by E· Eldon Deane

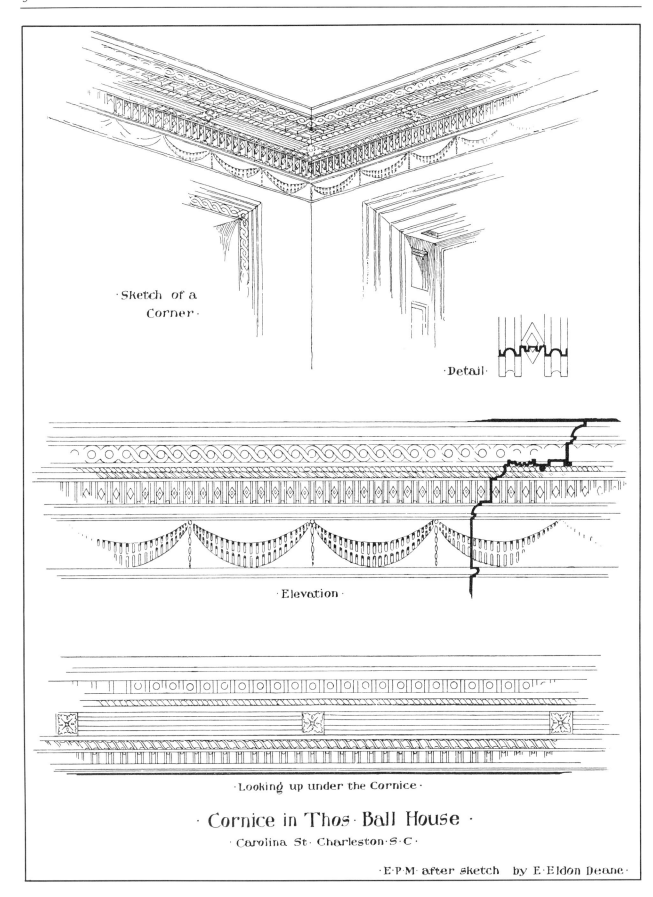

·Sketch of a
Corner·

·Detail·

·Elevation·

·Looking up under the Cornice·

· Cornice in Thos· Ball House ·
·Carolina St· Charleston·S·C·

·E·P·M· after sketch   by E·Eldon Deane·

ELLIOTT HOUSE, CHARLESTON,
SOUTH CAROLINA

that this they did because they could not very well help doing so, and while these good people have been dreaming of their family trees, the Northerners have been studiously pushing a way for their sons and daughters.

Among the pleasurable trips from Charleston, a visit to and a stay of a few days in old Georgetown—so intimately connected with the older families of that city—well repays one, and it is from there the trip through the Santee district is made. Situated as it is about sixty miles (as the crow flies) northeast and on the coast—or, more strictly, on Sampit Creek—at the junction of the Black and Waccamaw rivers, as they open into the sea, one should in these days make the journey in about two hours, whereas the trip consumes four or five hours. The first half of the journey is by the main line (Atlantic Coast Line) to Lane's Junction, taking you through St. Stephen's, across the Santee River, due north, and then, in the shakiest and dirtiest of makeshift railroad cars, you are jolted or joggled along to your destination, with a stop every five or eight minutes, now for a word between the conductor and some planter, who rides up to the crossing to pass the time of day; then to take on an odd bale of cotton; anon to embark a colored woman with a basket of eggs, or some woeful chickens; again we stop just to stretch our limbs, or for the engine to take water, and indeed so thirsty did that locomotive appear that at last I classed it as amphibious.

Dusty, hot, stifled, at last one emerges onto the platform of the Georgetown station, glad to incarcerate oneself again for a brief while inside an ancient omnibus, so long as one may be put down at some hotel—no, not at that lumber-barracks opposite the station; but away from the dusky crowd, in the old

town—and in a few minutes you are dumped onto the sidewalk at the "Windsor," and a genial landlord gives you a hearty welcome with extended hand. After some vigorous ablutions you are glad to hear the dinner bell, rung by a colored waiter—with a vigor only equaled by an English railway-porter's—on the piazza, right on the sidewalk. I fully expected the whole town to come up with a rush and recalled the parable of the five loaves and two small fishes amongst the multitude; but my fears were baseless. The company was limited, and suffice it that I found more hearty fare than at any hotel—not excepting that old stand-by, the "Charleston" of Charleston—in all my trip. Now, this was a little unpretentious one-horse-town hotel, but in the limited quarters designated "office" was a bookcase, and there was a complete edition of the *Encyclopaedia Americana* flanked at the one end by the *Holy Bible* and at the other by *Webster's Unabridged*, with various reference books, histories and commentaries on a lower shelf. Surely, many a more pretentious establishment might take a hint from this, the entirely unexpected. Nor was the privilege shirked, for many times I observed various drummers poring over encyclopaedia and dictionary, if not the Bible.

Georgetown divides its interests: there is the long main street with its modern storefronts of frame structure and pushing trade, much of it maintained by the Hebrew element, and, on the other hand, there is the restful quiet of the residential section, with a pictur-

A CHARLESTON HOUSE GATE

A CHARLESTON GATEWAY

esqueness and beauty only to be found where modern changes are eschewed. Its old houses conservatively preserved, though boasting little of architectural detail, fascinate you with the mere suggestiveness of their antiquity, of course accentuated with the Southern features. Spaciously laid out, with very wide streets or boulevards, old-time gardens, and reveling in the shade of fine old oaks, the memory recalls it as a dream of the past.

It is interesting here to notice the growth in plan of the older houses. The original rough log cabin of the country or pine woods, now transplanted into the precincts of a civilized community, assumes in the frame house of the same plan a more finished appearance. The outside chimney at one end, instead of being constructed of clay or short interlaced logs besmeared with clay, is now of brick. Presently on an enlarged scale, you have a hearth and chimney at either end, and anon a double story. The house is now divided by a narrow hall, with staircase in the rear. With increased prosperity and personal importance comes the piazza, first single, then double. Again, to better facilitate domestic requirements, an outbuilding is erected

MANIGAULT HOUSE, CHARLESTON,
SOUTH CAROLINA

FRIENDFIELD, NEAR GEORGETOWN, SOUTH CAROLINA

away from the house, and then a small covered gallery is needed to connect with the house. This, as the family quarters are found to be too limited, is closed in, and you have an L, and so on. You cannot very well attach this development to the larger houses, but it is noticeable in the dwellings of the laboring classes and of the colored element. In some of these cottages the walls are wainscoted to the ceiling, and here and there you come across a finely modeled door knocker or other suggestion of architectural and refined tastes. Some peeps into the interior of these primitive houses revealed scrupulous cleanliness and neatness; here and there evidences of good taste.

The old church, Prince George Winyard, is still, after nearly two hundred years, a specimen of beautiful brickwork in English bond and, with its quaint tower and massive arched window heads, embowered in trees, is a picture from any point of view. The old market, too, with its tower, built about 1840, is striking in its simplicity and, being the rendezvous of boatmen, skippers, townsmen, colored loafers and

looking up a dark alley

Rear View
PROSPECT HILL, ON THE WACCAMAW RIVER, SOUTH CAROLINA

ROBERT J. TURNBULL HOUSE, NEAR CHARLESTON, SOUTH CAROLINA

CHARLESTON POST OFFICE

the ever-present mule-cart, makes a curious picture to Northern eyes.

From Georgetown a visit was made to Friendfield, an old plantation-house about six or eight miles out in the woods, where the singular find of the pictured wall paper was made. The house was interesting in plan, but appeared to be rather a patchwork of additions. Strange to say, while I had heard of the name of this amongst other plantation-houses—so many of them burned—no one could give me any information about it, and only on the morning of my departure did I manage to reach it, and, so, had too little time to do justice to it.

Another trip that was as pleasureable as it was interesting was up the Waccamaw River (two or three miles wide), in a little rowboat, with a burly negro, half a dozen or more miles, to visit Prospect Hill, the old home of the Huger family, where La Fayette was welcomed and entertained on his second visit to this country. I believe, too, that Washington here paid a visit. After a couple of hours on the water, we pulled inshore and along a narrow canal to the landing, about a mile inland. The banks of this canal, which in the olden days were well preserved and kept, were a tangle of riotous vines and pampas grasses, sometimes overarching us, while on either side stretched the wide rice fields. From the landing a tortuous path led up the hill to the old house, embowered 'mid old oaks, a picture of sad decay. Evidences of a once richly cultivated garden were everywhere. Ivy climbed the walls and hid the old stone stairs to the piazza, with its wrought iron railing of quaint design. The house was of the simplest in plan, being divided by a wide hall from front to rear, the house being two rooms deep. Shown over it by a little colored boy, who seemed to tip-toe it everywhere and spoke in muffled whisper, the silence, with the everywhere apparent desolation, was so oppressive that only my limited time in which to get my sketching and measuring done kept me to my task. Afterward rambling around the estate, inspecting the different outhouses, smoke and baking houses and the site of the farm buildings—for that is all that remains—I was glad to come away, sick at heart in contemplating the ruthless transition from the days of its one-time prosperity and happiness.

The row back was a relief from the stifling heat and oppressiveness on shore, and though the little flat-bottomed cockleshell of a boat rocked a little too much in the tidal current midstream for one's entire confidence, the freshness was grateful, while it was interesting to take note of little things; for instance, the home of the alligator on the banks, and the genial exchange of "How d'ye do's" between my skipper and other boats' companies passing half a mile away, and, strange to say, just in an ordinary voice, which would be answered clearly and intelligibly on the instant. All this section of country was once a veritable garden of cultivation; first indigo, then rice and cotton and tobacco; and it was the proprietors of these plantations, with their fine old houses and retinues of servants, who helped to build up Charleston, which was their summer home. A colony of Huguenots, their family names today predominate, and of these names the present generation is justly proud.

Picture-Paper Room

FRIENDFIELD, GEORGETOWN, SOUTH CAROLINA

Picture-Paper Parlor

FRIENDFIELD, NEAR GEORGETOWN, SOUTH CAROLINA

One End of Picture-Paper Room

FRIENDFIELD, GEORGETOWN, SOUTH CAROLINA

One End of Picture-Paper Room
FRIENDFIELD, GEORGETOWN, SOUTH CAROLINA

NATHANIEL HEYWARD HOUSE — 1750 — EAST BAY STREET, CHARLESTON,
SOUTH CAROLINA

NATHANIEL RUSSELL HOUSE — c1785 — CHARLESTON, SOUTH CAROLINA

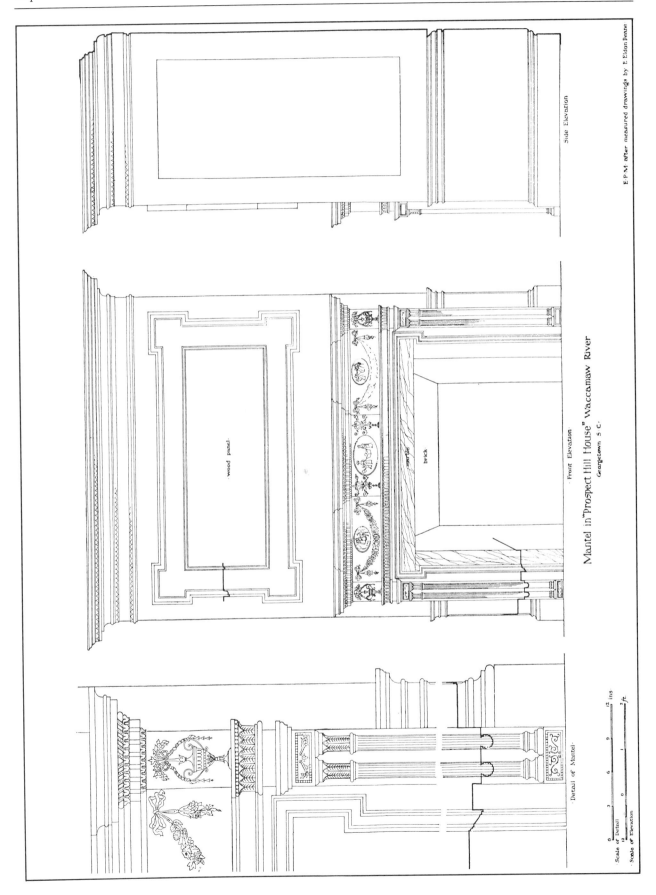

Side Elevation

wood panel.

marble

brick

Front Elevation

Detail of Mantel

Mantel in "Prospect Hill House" Waccamaw River
Georgetown S.C.

E.P.M. after measured drawings by E.Eldon Deane

Scale of Detail
Scale of Elevation

NATHANIEL HEYWARD HOUSE AND GATEWAY –1750– EAST BAY STREET, CHARLESTON, SOUTH CAROLINA

Prospect Hill
Plantation

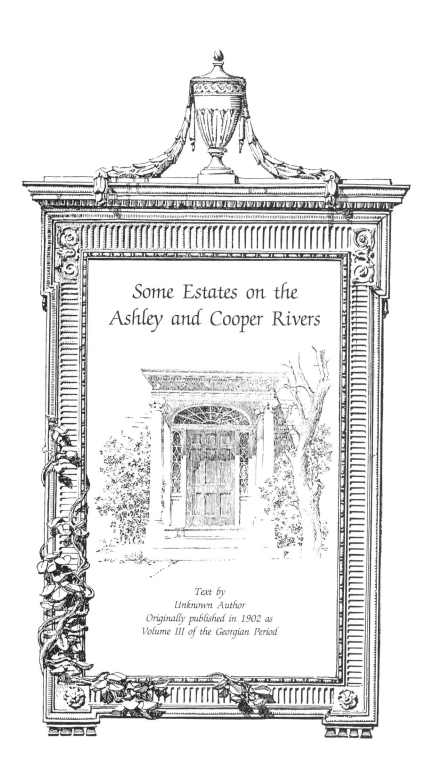

Some Estates on the
Ashley and Cooper Rivers

Text by
Unknown Author
Originally published in 1902 as
Volume III of the Georgian Period

Parlor Mantelpiece

BELVEDERE FARMHOUSE, ON THE COOPER RIVER, NEAR CHARLESTON,
SOUTH CAROLINA

SOME ESTATES ON THE ASHLEY AND COOPER RIVERS, SOUTH CAROLINA

DRAYTON Hall is the only family mansion on the Ashley River near Charleston which escaped the torch applied by Sherman's army. It also would have shared the common destiny but for the fact that the Drayton family was divided against itself, and Capt. Percival Drayton, of the United States Navy, a brother of Gen. Thomas S. Drayton, commander in the Confederate Army, and the then owner of Drayton Hall, was stationed outside the bar with the fleet that so long blockaded Charleston Harbor. Realizing the danger that threatened the family mansion he sent a special guard to protect it.

The estate, of which this fine old relic is a part, joins another equally celebrated, known as Magnolia on the Ashley. Both of these properties are entailed in the Drayton family, and, although they are now owned by distant cousins, were originally settled by father and son.

Thomas Drayton, the founder of the family, was one of the many Englishmen who came from the Barbadoes with Sir Thomas Yeamans. He received a grant from the Crown comprising several thousand acres, which he settled in 1761, calling the place Magnolia on the Ashley, because of the magnolia-grandiflora trees that grew there in natural abundance. In 1742, John Drayton, the eldest son of Thomas Drayton, and himself the father of William Henry Drayton, one of the distinguished men of the Revolution and the grandfather of John Drayton, a governor of South Carolina, built Drayton Hall on an adjoining tract.

The place takes its name from the family estate in Northamptonshire, England, and the hall itself cost ninety thousand dollars, all the materials being imported from England. It is still in excellent preservation, although unoccupied, and is built of red brick with columns of Portland marble. The staircase, man-tel and wainscot, which extends in quaint fashion from floor to ceiling, are of solid mahogany richly carved and paneled. Over the mantel are stationary carved frames for family portraits and heraldic devices; and the great fireplace is inlaid with antique colored tiles. To this day many stories are told of the dinners and balls held at Drayton Hall in the great old days, when the house would be ablaze with a thousand tapers, and carpets were laid down the staircases, front and back, and across the gardens, so the ladies might alight from their carriages and enter the hall without soiling their delicate slippers or the airy lace and satin of their robes.

Magnolia on the Ashley has been less fortunate than Drayton Hall, for its dwelling has been twice destroyed by fire, once during the Revolution, after which it was rebuilt, and later by Sherman's army. Its chief glory is now its gardens, which are among the finest in the world, and are visited annually by thousands of tourists. Their most picturesque feature is the display of azaleas in all shades and tints, crimson and pink, and blue and purple, with now and then a pure white bush. The gardens are in perfect preservation. Smooth walks wind through rich wildernesses of color; placid lakes mirror a thousand different hues; great live-oak trees are weighted down with moss; and walls of rhododendrons and banks of golden banksias lend their gay colors to the brilliant picture.

Before the azaleas begin to decline, the camellia-japonica trees burst into flower and delight the onlooker with perfections undreamed of. There are six acres of these, white and pink and mottled, which grow in clusters of great cone-shaped bushes, scentless and cold, but exquisite to behold in the tropical luxuriance of these unequaled gardens. A little later as the spring advances the magnolia trees come to blossom.

A Garden Walk
MAGNOLIA ON THE ASHLEY, SOUTH CAROLINA

Then, indeed, the place is an enchanted spot worthy of a queen in state. The waters of the Atlantic ebb and flow languorously in the river, where on each bank the lush grass grows. The air is heavy with fragrance, and the great trees loom in stately masses, sheltering their proud blossoms amid the cool shadows of waxy leaves. In the midst of all this floral munificence stands the tomb of the Draytons', where six generations are sleeping.

The camellia japonica, by the way, is one of the show flowers of the lowlands of South Carolina, where, though not indigenous, it reaches even greater perfection than in the land of its birth. One of the finest camellia-japonica trees in the world is at Middleton Place, on the Ashley River, not far from Drayton Hall. The house of Middleton Place is now in ruins, having been one of the many burned by Sherman's army; but the gardens give evidence, even at this late day, of the great perfection they attained at one time. They were laid out in 1750 by Michaux, a celebrated landscape-gardener who is associated with early American history. He did considerable fine work in and around Charleston, and at one time had charge of Sir William Middleton's gardens at Shrubland, Suffolk, which are celebrated, even in England, for their extent and beauty. One of the things planted at Middleton Place by Michaux was a camellia-japonica bush which thrived prodigiously, quite outclassing in perfection any others planted at the same time, or since, in fact.

It so happened that some fifty or sixty years ago, Mr. William Middleton, on one of his visits to England, had a permit to inspect the gardens of Windsor Castle. The head-gardener showed him through all the green-houses, pointing out first one, then another of the choice specimens there. Finally, he led him to a house apart from the others, in the center of which was a small camellia bush showing some twenty or thirty blooms.

"There!" said the head-gardener with pride. "Is not that beautiful? Is it not superb—unique?"

"It is very pretty, indeed," said Mr. Middleton, or words to that effect.

"I consider it the choicest specimen in the entire

Arthur Middleton Tomb
MIDDLETON PLACE, ASHLEY RIVER, SOUTH CAROLINA

collection," said the head-gardener. "Do you not agree with me?"

"Yes," replied Mr. Middleton, "I think perhaps it is."

The gardener was chagrined at the evident lack of enthusiasm on the part of the American, and pressed him further.

"But isn't it the finest bush of the kind you ever saw?"

"Well, no," replied Mr. Middleton. "I have in my garden at home a camellia-japonica tree that is twenty feet high, and when I left it had on it, as near as I can calculate, about four thousand blooms."

"Why, bless my soul!" exclaimed the Queen's gardener, "you must be a Middleton of Middleton Place, in the Carolinas. We know of that tree. It was planted by Michaux in 1750, and is one of the botanical wonders."

Nature *is* in a bountiful mood on the banks of the Ashley River, and occasionally takes it into her head there to do her very best, as in this instance, and again in the case of a giant live-oak tree in the pasture of Drayton Hall which has grown to enormous size and perfection, and was pronounced by Professor Sargent,

the botanist, the most beautiful tree of its kind in the world. This live oak, in common with all trees near the South Carolina coast, is draped with tillandsia, that peculiar mosslike growth peculiar to lowland forests near the Southern Sea.

The wonderful productiveness of the Ashley River region made it formerly the seat of the rich cavalier planters of South Carolina. The Izard family resided near The Oaks, near Goose Creek Church, which was settled in 1678. Crowfield was, until 1754, another residence of the Middleton family. Ashley Hall was the home of the Bull family. Across, on Cooper River were many other splendid old homes: Yeamans Hall was built there by Sir Thomas Yeamans about 1680.

"The house," says an early chronicler, "was of brick, said to have been brought over from England. It was a two-story structure with basement, almost square, with an extension in the rear, and a broad veranda at the front. The interior was elegantly finished. The walls were painted in panels representing landscapes, and hung with tapestries. The large fireplaces were lined with Dutch tiles in blue and white, depicting Biblical scenes. At the time of my visit the house had not yet been burned, and remains of this former

Drayton Tomb
MAGNOLIA ON THE ASHLEY — 1671 — SOUTH CAROLINA

beauty could be seen in the broken cornices and hand-some mouldings around the rooms. Entering from the front you came into a large hall, with an immense chimney-place in one corner; from this hall led doors communicating with four rooms, another door gave access to the rear of the house, from which a staircase led to the upper story. Between the walls of the upper and lower stories of an extension in the rear of the building was situated a secret chamber, access to which was had through a trapdoor concealed in a closet.

"This house was constructed with a view to defense in case of any attack from hostile Indians. In the base-ment the walls are pierced at intervals on all sides with loopholes for firearms, as is also the wall of the stair-case leading to the upper floor. In the basement once could be seen the entrance to an underground tunnel, arched with brick, which led to an opening near the creek, thus affording a means of escape for the family if hard pressed. There was a haunted chamber where the ghost of a stately dame, arrayed in costly brocade, was wont to appear."

Mulberry Towers, the home of the Broughton fam-ily, commonly called The Mulberry, is also on the Cooper River; likewise Belvedere, and the ruins of Medway, the home of Landgrave Thomas Smith.

At the time of the Revolution social life on the Ashley and Cooper rivers was conducted on a splendid scale, equaled only by that of the gentleman planters of the James River. The English who settled that sec-tion, by the way, the Harrisons, the Byrds, the Carters and the Berkeleys, were of the same political and social class as those who composed the society of the Ashley and Cooper rivers, and their homes for the most part, though on the whole less architectural because of the inability to secure skilled labor, represent the same general ideas of construction.

Parlor Doorway
BELVEDERE FARMHOUSE — 1810 — ON THE COOPER RIVER, NEAR CHARLESTON,
SOUTH CAROLINA

DRAYTON HALL—1740—ON THE ASHLEY RIVER, NEAR CHARLESTON, SOUTH CAROLINA

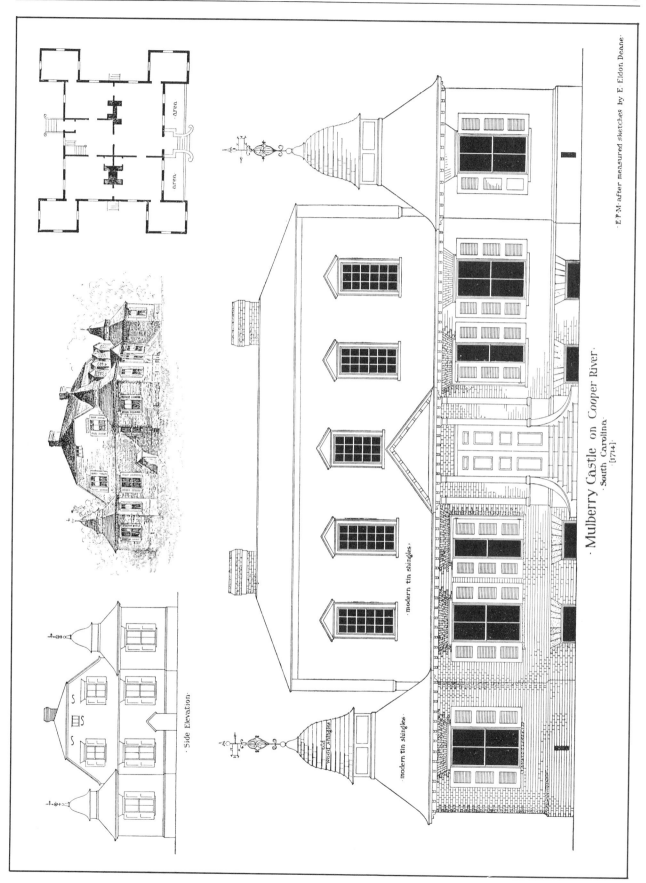

· Side Elevation ·

· modern tin shingles ·

· modern tin shingles ·

· old wood shingles ·

· Mulberry Castle · on · Cooper River ·
· South Carolina ·
[1714]

· E·P·M· after measured sketches by E. Eldon Deane ·

BELVEDERE FARMHOUSE — 1810 — ON THE COOPER RIVER, NEAR CHARLESTON, SOUTH CAROLINA

Millford, in the High
Hill of Santee, S.C.

Text by
Olive F. Gunby
Originally published in 1902 as
Volume III of the Georgian Period

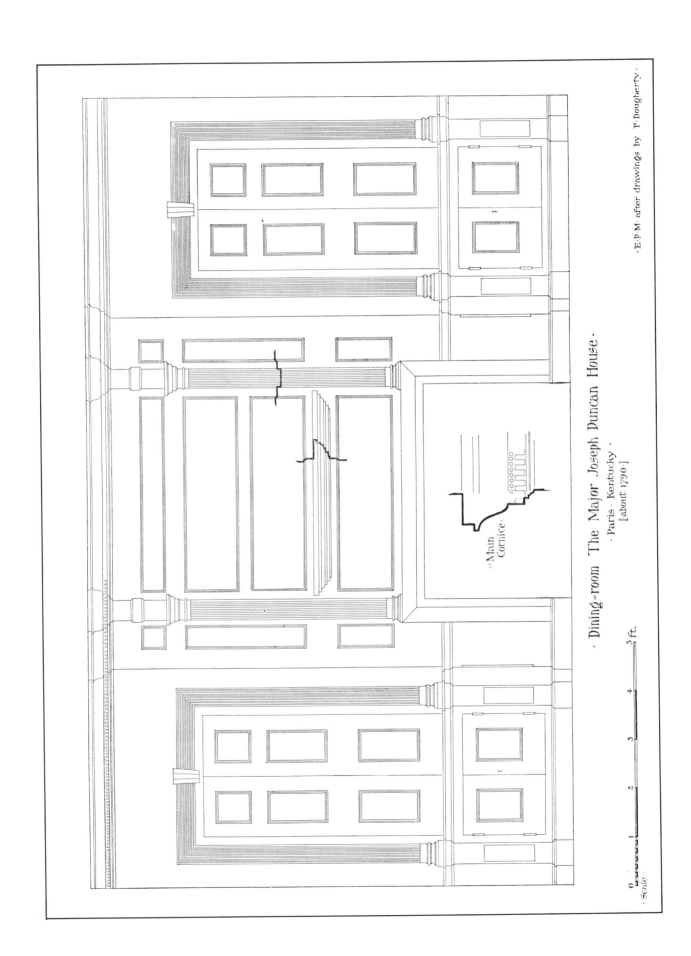

· Dining-room The Major Joseph Duncan House ·

· Paris · Kentucky ·

[about 1790·]

· Main Cornice ·

· E·P·M· after drawings by P· Dougherty ·

· Scale ·   0   1   2   3   4   5 ft.

MILLFORD, IN THE HIGH HILL OF SANTEE, SOUTH CAROLINA

NOWHERE in the South is there a country-seat more strikingly individual than the Manning homestead in the High Hills of Santee, South Carolina. Certainly, few plantation-houses were ever built with more care or at greater cost. The architect was induced to come from New York for the sole purpose of putting up an ideal dwelling in this rural spot, where every brick and stone, every bit of framing and decoration, must be got from foreign parts, freighted ninety miles up the Santee River from Charleston, and hauled over crude roads, up steep hills, to the site. The South Carolina Railroad, pioneer of its class in the United States, was only five or six years old when the foundations of the house were laid — and the railroad passed nowhere near it. The river was the only practical means of transportation from the outside world. All the skilled laborers and decorators who aided in the building had to make long journeys by private conveyance to reach the spot. Nevertheless, the house, as it stands today, would win notice on a stately city avenue. And, all solitary in its wildwood setting, the superb, if lonely, prospect outspread before it but gives additional worth and emphasis.

The building was more than two years in course of construction and is said to have cost its founder $100,000. Full seventy feet long by forty-five feet wide and three stories in height, with a finely columned Grecian porch, the mansion pleases the eye, not only as to substantialness, but in grace of outline. Although the builder had a liking for the ornate and sumptuous, as is proved by the statuary niched in the walls and the devices ornamenting the great pillars which support the porch roof, only so much decoration as comports with the style of architecture was permitted to appear. The planters from the Georgetown section, who had dwellings in the high, dry plateau of the Sand Hills and had lived there successively since early settlement days, would have constructed fine homes for themselves long before 1830 had conditions been different. But up to that time, lime, a chief ingredient in structures built of stone or brick, was procured only with much difficulty and at expense. Transportation from sections where bricks were made was a serious issue, and as timber was plenty, the residents had wooden houses, planned on an ample scale, but crude, from the modern standpoint, planing-mills being few and but newly introduced in the country.

In the first decade after the Revolution houses comfortable and pleasing in structure were to be found within a half mile of each other in this favored district. Even before that time a good classical school and a circulating library were supported there. And when Governor Manning erected this sumptuous new dwelling on the family lands in the Sand Hills the neighborhood could furnish abundant society, descendants and connections of the original settlers, people from Louisiana and Virginia, having built homes there, attracted by the unusually fine climate and fertile lands, people of cultivated tastes, versed in the arts and enjoyments of life.

The Manning House is unused now, although in good preservation. With the passing of slavery, the tillage of the lands and the care of the extensive grounds were too costly to be worth while. The visitor's footsteps echo emptily on the handsome tiled flooring of the broad veranda. Seldom are the garden walks traversed save by the pickaninnies, the little grandchildren of the caretaker. Occasionally neighbors visit the spot to get some rare plant or flowering shrub for transplanting to their gardens, or else to look in

MISCELLANEOUS WROUGHT IRONWORK

through some gaping window blind at the furnishings within. But entertainments were frequent there up to the time that the Civil War shut down on an exceptionally prosperous community. The great drawing rooms, with their full-length mirrors and artistic decoration, often held gatherings of distinguished and interesting people. The Christmas house-parties were famous. For ten days at that season all occupations, even politics, were laid aside and jollification ruled. Every plantation thereabout had its own band of trained fiddlers, banjo and bone players, enthusiastic musicians who sought to outdo one another in vim and efficiency when the dances were held at their respective houses. Sometimes the minuet and lancers would be danced with representatives of four distinct generations in a single set, so thoroughly did the old folks and the young unite in innocent pastime.

The old lodgekeeper at the porter's lodge, which yet stands by the entrance gate, could tell of the gay parties he was wont to let in and out of the Millford grounds by day and night in the happy days. But he, along with a host of family retainers, is elsewhere now seeking a living. Only one ex-slave does the honors of the home-place, one Benjamin Pleasants, body-servant to the late Governor. The old man has little to do as guardian, for the neighborhood is almost as deserted now as it was once populous. The fine mahogany tables and chairs, the rare old candlesticks, the Japanese curios and articles of virtu brought from foreign lands that are yet within the house are safe behind unlocked doors, for only a simple-minded tenantry, who would not know what to do with them if they stole them, live nearby, and the location is far off the track of tourists and dealers in antiquities.

The old body-servant has had romances in his life. Once, in the early 1840s, he attended his master to Canada. The journey was an undertaking in those days, and Ben was regarded as a hero by the other house-servants because of the chance to make it. While in Canada some zealous abolitionists kidnapped Ben, and secreted him until Governor Manning had ceased to make search and had started back home. When they told Ben that he was free and need never work again for any but his own interests, Ben, being thick-headed and warm-hearted, was greatly distressed. He kept his own counsel, but resolved to work his way back to his master, no matter how long it took. He got back after months of hardship, and great was the rejoicing in the Millford household on the day he appeared, safe and sound. There was frolic and feasting in the big brick kitchen-quarters, and numerous were the "paroles" applied for by Ben's friends on neighboring plantations, anxious to get over to the Manning place and see for themselves that he was back, looking and acting just as before.

Politics was a strong interest with all the families allied with this family seat. The inmates could get up a notable company at any time, just among their own relatives. As though the high hills over which these men ruled instigated in them a spirit of dominance, no little corner of the state ever contributed so many leaders in war, in legislative assembly and public matters. Governor Manning himself was the second of his name to fill the gubernatorial chair. He married, first, Miss Hampton, a fine woman and a fine fortune, and at her death allied himself with a distinguished Virginia family. His mother was of a family whose habit it was to be governors, and she held the relationship of being respectively the daughter, sister, mother and aunt of a governor of South Carolina, three Richardsons having at various times filled that office since 1802, and all descendants of that Richard Richardson who ably seconded General Marion in his military manoeuvres conducted from Snow's Island, just across the country from the Santee. Immediately after the Civil War, Governor Manning was elected to the United States Senate, but evil times then prevailed. The carpetbaggers had other views for that particular Senatorial honor and prevented the Governor from taking his seat.

The old home-site has several times shared in epoch-making scenes. Lord Rawdon camped on the spot in June, 1781, when he made his long, forced march from Charleston for the relief of the garrison at Ninety-Six. Lord Cornwallis had also made the place a visit on his way to the battle of Camden, the year previous. A springhouse, canopied with a dome patterned after St. Paul's Cathedral, in London, now marks the spot where the British soldiery got such clear, cold water in that burning midsummer time. The site is just across the river from Fort Motte of romantic memory, and was in direct line with the other British posts along the Santee Valley from Charleston. General Sumter and his men passed and repassed Millford on their expeditions against these posts; as fast as Lord Rawdon managed to relieve one fort, the Americans appearing before another. It was to these Sand Hills that Marion retired in the winters to recruit his little, hard-fought army, knowing that there they would be singularly exempt from the cold of the lowlands. Marion and Sumter were natives of this district, and understood its characteristics. Once Sumter, with one hundred and fifty horsemen, plunged into the Santee near this point, and gained the opposite bank successfully to the astonishment of the British, who dared not follow. To ride, and swim, and shoot at one hundred and fifty yards were habitual with the Sand Hill dwellers.

The black waters of the Wateree, which river has a swamp three miles deep, and the clay-colored waters of the Congaree, come together, and form the Santee at a point a few miles above the Millford landing. The confluence makes a goodly spectacle. And farther on the yellow waters prevail, the broad Santee preserving that tinge all its ninety-odd miles to the sea.

Once again, in April, 1865, Millford felt the impress of hostile footfall: one of Sherman's aides took the house for headquarters, while the raiding troops were passing, and while that other great army of contrabands was got under way. Then the ladies of the family sat at the upper windows and watched the rabble and tumult without, and beheld their slave people passing on and away to a new era of existence. The commanding officer was a man of discrimination. He admired the stately plantation-home and preserved order about it to the best of his ability. It is twenty years since the place has been actually lived in. With changing times the family interests have centered elsewhere, the daughters marrying into other communities, the sons engaging in city businesses. No one has time or means to live at leisure in the old home when so much around and without it has changed, and so, although the weather has made no inroads as yet, and the superb climate of the Hills is as enticing as ever, the place is left to itself, mute witness to the tastes and requisites of a time that is gone.

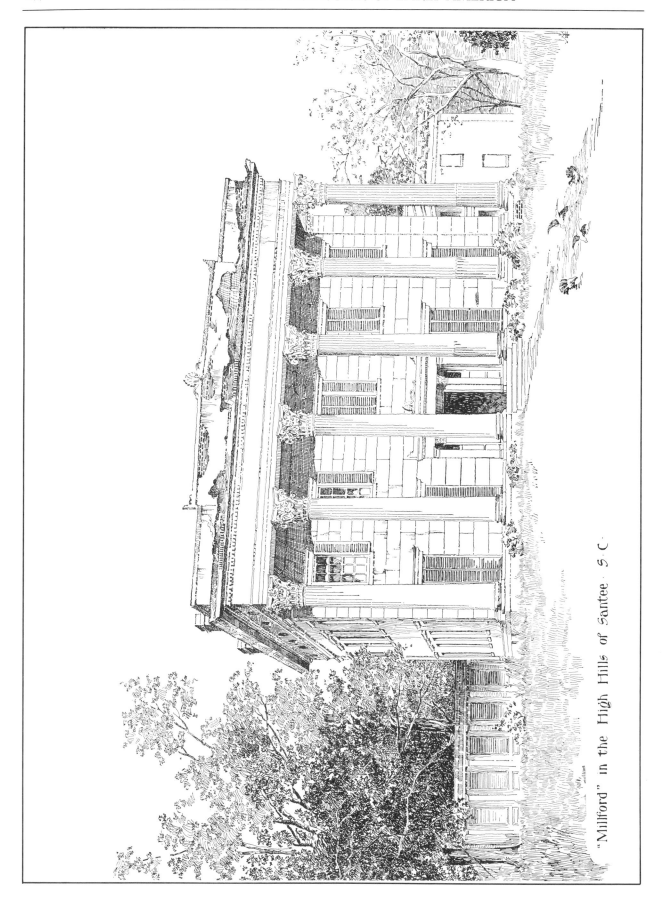

"Millford" in the High Hills of Santee · S·C·

De Saussure Homestead,
Near Camden, South Carolina

Text by
Olive F. Gunby
Originally published in 1902 as
Volume III of the Georgian Period

DE SAUSSURE HOUSE, SOUTH BATTERY, CHARLESTON, SOUTH CAROLINA

THE DE SAUSSURE HOMESTEAD, NEAR CAMDEN, SOUTH CAROLINA

ANOTHER South Carolina mansion that deserves record is Lausanne, the De Saussure homestead, just outside of Camden. Although this place was sold some years ago, and alterations made in it with the view of entertaining Northern tourists, its original character was too strong to be obliterated. And its antiquity and first existence as a private home designed to fill the wants of a hospitable, large-minded owner is stamped from garret to cellar. Camden is one of the oldest communities in the country, and Lausanne was built for the De Saussure whom Washington appointed Director of the Mint, and under whose jurisdiction the first gold coins used in the United States were minted. He afterward became Chancellor. Lausanne was for a long period the showplace of Camden and the chosen home where the distinguished people who visited the town on the Wateree were sure to find entertainment. The place was celebrated for its beautiful grounds, many imported shrubs and trees being planted there, the site being one of exceptional advantage for the growth of roses and native flowers.

Lafayette was entertained at this homestead when he visited Camden in 1825 in order to take part in the unveiling of the monument to De Kalb, the illustrious German in the service of France who so generously aided the Americans' cause, and was the hero of the Camden fight.

When the proprietor of Lausanne, in 1795, resigned from the directorship of the Mint, and returned to Carolina to practice law, he persuaded Washington, his personal friend, to sit to Rembrandt Peale for a portrait to be hung on the walls at the Camden house. This portrait, an extraordinarily good likeness, for Washington sat patiently to please his friend, was painted, and adorned the morning-room at Lausanne many years. The likeness was so perfect, it is said, that Lafayette, when he first beheld it, saluted and exclaimed in French, "My friend, God guard you."

Lausanne received much attention at the hands of freebooters and raiders of both armies towards the close of the Civil War: this because of the reputed wealth of the owners, and the belief that much plate and treasure was buried on the premises. A number of good pictures hung upon the walls, many of them authenticated portraits of the members of the De Saussure family, painted by noted artists. The careless soldiers, when Lausanne was being sacked, amused themselves by sticking their bayonets through these portraits and other pictures. A soldier who was idly lunging at everything on his side of the house, and had let the daylight through two or three framed pictures, suddenly felt his arm arrested by a comrade, and was warned to notice whom he was about to slash next. Even this vandal had compunctions about damaging the "Father of his Country," and the portrait was left unhurt.

Eleven years after the war the descendants of the Chancellor who had made Lausanne their home for over eighty years were in sore straits. The cherished acres and associations alike had to be given up. The Washington portrait was shipped to a collector in Philadelphia and sold, and the beautiful home-place was bought by a lady with an eye to the good business it would bring as an inn, because of the very historical and antique flavor that hangs about it and its belongings.

Gates and Servants' Quarters

DE SAUSSURE HOUSE — 1830 — CHARLESTON, SOUTH CAROLINA

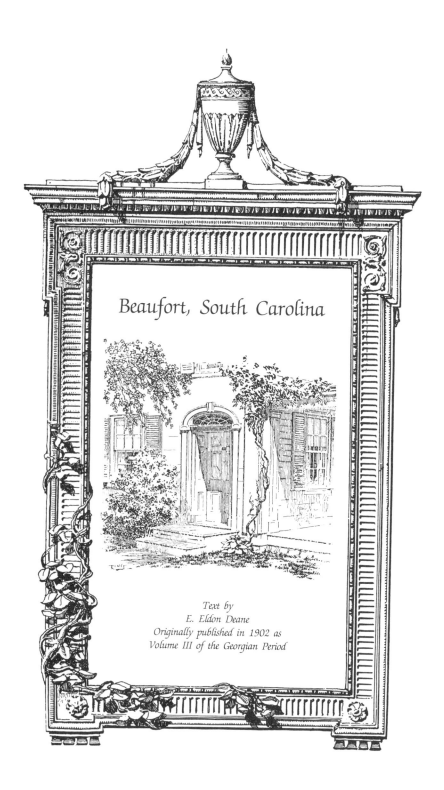

Beaufort, South Carolina

Text by
E. Eldon Deane
Originally published in 1902 as
Volume III of the Georgian Period

Rear
BULL-PRINGLE (MILES BREWTON) HOUSE, CHARLESTON, SOUTH CAROLINA

BEAUFORT, SOUTH CAROLINA:
AN ISLAND CAPITAL

AFTER a stay in dull and tedious commercial Savannah, the little sea-trip to Beaufort was a welcome change and full of interest. Sailing about noon, the little steamer slipped slowly down the river, past the old wharves and warehouses and the newer docks of the cotton-freighted steamers, which afford more picturesqueness than any other feature in the city, for, be it remembered, the city being built on a high bluff, on the southern bank, the warehouses and offices which line the edge of the bluff, while to the south presenting a front of only two or three stories, in the rear descend sheer seven or eight stories, frowning like precipices with their granite walls and heavy stacks of chimneys; and the winding cuts from the higher level to the cobblestoned street flanking the wharves have an ancient and somewhat military appearance. After passing out of the river and by Tybee Island and lighthouse, the "Nahant" of Savannah, we take a northerly but not an open-sea course, as a stranger half expects, zigzagging through an endless series of islands, all characteristically similar, low and flat, but looking deliciously cool, fringed with the ever-present Georgia palms, and tall salt grasses, so bleached in the sun that they vie with the silver strand in whiteness. Here and there a white cottage or some farm-steading breaks the solitariness, and stands in relief against some distant woodland, while a column of smoke from some camping party may be seen pirouetting skyward.

There was a merry party of colored folks aboard, and their hilarity was infectious. Many of them were looking forward to a cake-walk on the morrow night, and were dressed in their Sunday best. One little dandy, in patent leathers, polished his shoes no less than four times that afternoon. A party of young women were discussing the vagaries of a too amorous father. "So you poppa gone mahyid again." "Sho, my poppa done bring home a new step-momma, an' I ain't gwine to stan' it. He don't count anyway." "Well," exclaims a companion, "if my poppa were to bring home a new step-momma, I'd kill him." Whether disaster followed the father in question or not, the incident was soon forgotten in the interest aroused by the setting out from the shore of one of the islands of a boat which met us and took off a number of our colored contingent amid screams of greeting and farewell, and the promise to meet on the morrow night. And so on, ever and anon, a boat would pull out to us in mid-stream and take on a few passengers and various freight, not forgetting many flasks of vile whiskey. It was the same experience as on the canals in Santee. Many, many times we stopped to supply some boat-load with soft wood (to be used as torches at night in the raid on the rice-birds), or grain, but most often with a number of "sealed packages" of whiskey, and away the boat's-crew would pull back to their eyrie through some inlet in the tall pampas grasses fringing the islands. Then we stopped at some military post, where a number of officers and men in khaki uniform were at the pier-end to take all in and be taken in by many critical glances of the fair sex. About six o'clock we reached Port Royal, the naval station, and there discharged a good deal of freight, conspicuous amongst which were some ample cases of Moët & Chandon, to enliven the dull tedium of officialdom separated from home ties. After inspecting the new dry-dock there, we went aboard again and pursued our journey for the four or five miles more that brought us to Beaufort. As the evening darkened the full moon rose, and, with a sky of deep turquoise, the water without a ripple and reflecting the sky, as we neared the town, where from the

BAY STREET, BEAUFORT, SOUTH CAROLINA

Door Head
FRANZ HOUSE, BEAUFORT, SOUTH CAROLINA

Door Head
MOUNT BRISTOL, BEAUFORT,
SOUTH CAROLINA

TABBY-BUILT CABINS, ST. CATHERINE'S ISLAND, COAST OF GEORGIA

OLD COLLEGE BUILDING, BEAUFORT,
SOUTH CAROLINA

MOUNT BRISTOL, BEAUFORT,
SOUTH CAROLINA

South Doorway

ST. HELENA'S, BEAUFORT, SOUTH CAROLINA

deep shadow of heavy foliage peeped many old and galleried houses, silvered by the moonlight, and all again mirrored in the glassy waters, there was presented a picture indelibly impressed on one's memory. Beaufort, the dreamy, silent, quaint, with gardens redolent of opopanax and many odorous shrubs. The very hotel was an old-time planter's mansion, and from it, after registering, a voyage of discovery was in order, a trip that promised much and delighted the eye, and although a subsequent and closer inspection failed to unearth much in the way of architectural and decorative detail, yet as a group of old-time houses and picturesque streets there was sufficient to make the old town well worthy of the visit.

Beaufort was the summer home of the planters, who came in May and left about November 15th for their plantations. The houses were built accordingly with an eye to air and space, with cool verandas overlooking the water, or bay, which here surrounds three-quarters of the town. Here families well known to each other intermingled year by year and gave themselves over to boating, bathing and fishing, and a good time generally, through the summer months. As a rule, these summer houses were not built as solidly or with such complete accommodations as the plantation mansions, and here noticeably absent are the extensive slave or servant quarters, so that it is evident that only a limited number of domestics was brought down with the

family and resided in the house. The details of cornices and mantels, and the wooden finish generally, have a family likeness, and are peculiar to the locality. The old Baptist parsonage and the old Elliott House are particularly so, as also the old Franz House, from the upper veranda of which La Fayette addressed the people of the town below in the street. In the Fuller House, on Bay Street, of which the double portico is given in a sketch, we have tabby-built walls, very solid, and to which the slender portico carried up the two stories gives relief from the severity of outline. The staircase is interesting in its double-return flight from the first central landing. This house is a type, with its portico, of several others in the town. There are also some creditable mantels, and the cornices are good; but in these houses, as in all the South, amplitude seems everywhere to have had prime consideration.

In one of the gardens I noticed a very medley of strange-shaped beds, star, oval, round, octagonal and crescent, each edged with a border of rounded stones, after the manner of the garden of the Bull-Pringle House in Charleston, with winding walks between and a little pool and fountain. But what is observable in the Southern gardens is the lack of moisture, and such lawns as one sees in the North are not to be found. The grass is stubby, strong and thick bladed, and it is in the shrubbery and vines that the gardens excel, and produce such languorous beauty.

A beautiful section of the town is what is called "the point," surrounded by water, and here the old houses, with their accompaniments of great oaks with their long wandering branches and dark foliage, afford some marvellous silhouettes of an evening. Indeed, Beaufort should be an artist's paradise, so full is it of the picturesque, mixed with a bewitching suggestion of antiquity.

Of the two old churches, St. Helena's is the Episcopal, of which the townspeople are justly proud. Standing in a great churchyard, with entrances on three

OLD BRICK TOMB, BEAUFORT,
SOUTH CAROLINA

Stair Landing
BEARDSLEY HOUSE, BEAUFORT, SOUTH CAROLINA

Sea Island Hotel
Beaufort S.C.

On the Point
Beaufort S.C.

sides, full of old tombs and family burial-plots, walled in with low brick walls, and interspersed with magnificent trees, it is the central attraction to visitors, and, contrary to the general sentiment, there are many of the townspeople who delight just to walk there, so beautiful and quiescent are the winding paths amid so many flowering and odorous shrubs. While the interior has been modernized, the exterior is unchanged, and retains all its original features, with the exception of the bell-tower, which has, I believe, been burned once or twice, and reconstructed without being properly finished. In the churchyard is an old brick tomb, and the story goes that the tenant before his demise was so fearful of being buried alive, and of suffocation, that after building his burial vault he made a stipulation that when he was laid away there should be placed beside his coffin, whose lid was to be left unscrewed, a jug of water and a loaf of bread; and this was done, and food and drink were kept there until such time as any possible reawakening was out of the question. These old burial vaults are peculiar in their form, as will be seen from the sketches of the one in question and also of one in the colonial cemetery in Savannah. They are literally houses (gabled houses) of the dead, and their roofs of brick often sag inwards from their weight. With vines creeping over them they

are often quite pretty. The old Baptist church, nearly coeval with its neighbor, St. Helena's, is interesting in its way, but of an ordinary type.

After a week in Beaufort I was loth to leave. There one is conscious of the very antithesis of the modern spirit of rush, and crowding, and haste. In times of business pressure and overburdening cares, it is positively soothing to let one's thoughts travel to and stay in such a place as Beaufort. But, alas! this will not last long, for already there is a big modern hotel contracted for under a Boston architect, and the old homes are being sought after and bought, and being changed to suit modern ideas and tastes.

Thus the entering wedge of modern and so-called advanced civilization is forcing its way in; but it will take a long time to modernize sleepy old Beaufort, though not so long to depreciate its present quiet picturesqueness.

There is an old hostelry now, once an old planter's house, that thoroughly expresses the spirit of the place. My host is a character, and a most genial and kindly one. Everything that can be done to make the guest happy is done, and in the Sea Island Hotel will be found a true home for the wayfarer, better than any gorgeous modern hotel can supply, for the reason that in it you are made one of the family.

Dining Room Mantelpiece
FULLER HOUSE, BEAUFORT, SOUTH CAROLINA

ELLIOTT HOUSE, BEAUFORT, SOUTH CAROLINA

·Room in the Beardsley·House· [Old Elliott House] ·Beaufort· S·C·

·Detail of Cornice·

Staircase
FULLER HOUSE, BEAUFORT, SOUTH CAROLINA

Porch
FULLER HOUSE, BEAUFORT, SOUTH CAROLINA

East Gateway
ST. HELENA'S CHURCHYARD, BEAUFORT, SOUTH CAROLINA

South Gateway
ST. HELENA'S CHURCHYARD, BEAUFORT, SOUTH CAROLINA

ST. HELENA'S CHURCH, BEAUFORT, SOUTH CAROLINA

DAISY BANK, ON THE SANTEE CANAL,
BEAUFORT, SOUTH CAROLINA

HOUSES OF BEAUFORT, SOUTH CAROLINA

Rear
FULLER HOUSE, BEAUFORT, SOUTH CAROLINA

French Santee, South Carolina

Text by
C. R. S. Horton
Originally published in 1902 as
Volume III of the Georgian Period

· South Front: "El Dorado" South Santee River·

FRENCH SANTEE, SOUTH CAROLINA

ABOUT forty miles north of Charleston, and some fifteen miles south of the quaint old city of Georgetown lies the "Santee River region," one of the earliest settled portions of South Carolina. Much of the architecture there is old and interesting, and some of it is quite unique.[1]

This section of the state is but little known to the public, but maintains a quaint Old World existence of its own; yet prior to the Revolution it was second to no other part of South Carolina in social importance, for the tax returns of that period show that over five thousand negro slaves were kept busy in the Santee swamps, and that the planters of that region had by that time acquired affluence, and in many instances great wealth. The old houses of this locality are seldom simple in design, as the agricultural pursuits of their builders, and their present remoteness from modern progress, would lead one to expect them to be, but are planned more or less after the ideals of the French and English aristocracy, with great guest-chambers, spacious dining rooms and, not infrequently, a ballroom; for two things governed their erection—the desired comfort of their occupants and the wish to meet the demands of social life as it existed among the rich rice planters of the "Santee River region." The sleeping-rooms were spacious, well provided with closets and well lighted. Almost invariably the houses had wide verandas at the back and front and were well situated. They were, in fact, roomy abodes well adapted to the climate and they represent a mode of life, once typical, that has largely passed away in the far South of the United States. Little remains now, even in the roman-tic Santee region, to witness to that life but these old houses—falling year after year more and more into disrepair—where a few descendants of Huguenot planters and Revolutionary soldiers cling fondly to the traditions of their ancient dwellings.

The Santee region proper is that entire tract of land through which the Santee River flows, but the particular portion now referred to lies between the north and south branches of the river. About twenty miles from its mouth the Santee forks, forming two wide yellow streams (with a delta of increasing width between) by means of which it empties itself into the sea. This delta, which is really a triangular inland island, inasmuch as it is surrounded on two sides by the Santee and on the third by the sea, and the low-lying lands on either bank, having been enriched from time to time by alluvial deposits from frequent overflows, were once the richest rice-lands in the South. At that period immense crops of grain were realized at the highest values, peace and plenty filled the land, and the fine old houses were furnished with every comfort and supplied with retinues of thoroughly trained servants. In the winter they were filled with guests, but the first breath of summer found them deserted, for the curse of this locality, as of all other low-lying sections in the South, is intermittent fever. To escape it, the planters of the Santee region took their families to Pineville,[2] a village now in ruins, which formerly occupied a high ridge of piney land two miles south of the Santee Swamp, and five miles from the river.

A long summer at Pineville was an ideal existence. Being all Huguenot planters of the Santee the inhabitants were all social equals, and all Episcopalians. Furthermore, they were all more or less related by intermarriage. Naturally they met without consciousness of social inferiority, and indulged in similar social habits, which, by the way, were typical of the people and the

---

[1] The materials used in construction were almost invariably English brick and cypress, in which the fertile swamps of the Santee region abound, and which, probably, accounts for the fact that, even in their half-abandoned state, the houses are so well preserved. Cypress, as is generally known, is one of the most durable of woods, being at the same time straight-grained, soft, and easily worked, and, therefore, invaluable for carpentry. Instances are known of doors and posts of cypress that have lasted 1,100 years.

[2] Pineville was established in 1794 and abandoned in 1819.

OLD WAMBORO (ST. JAMES'S) CHURCH—
1768—FRENCH SANTEE, SOUTH CAROLINA

period. Breakfast at Pineville was commonly served at sunrise, after which each planter went on horseback to visit his plantation, taking care to arrive there after the sun was an hour or so high and all danger of infection passed until after sundown. At one o'clock dinner was served and a portion of the afternoon that followed was devoted to sleep. Every piazza at Pineville was furnished with long benches, and upon these rude resting-places the gentlemen of the house indulged in the luxury of a siesta. The afternoon nap over, tea and hot cakes were served. Seven o'clock supper closed the day, for which every one made a formal toilet, just as in England they dress for dinner. Then social life began, visits being made and received while the entertainers and those entertained sat upon verandas in the soft starlight, laughing and chatting, while great bonfires sparkled and sputtered before them, making bright the dark yard. It was the custom at Pineville to light these bonfires as soon as heavy dusk set in, and they were the unfailing features of every evening's festivities.

Riding, hunting, fishing, dancing and visiting were the amusements at Pineville, and who would ask for any better? The season closed every year with a Jockey Club Ball, after which, the much desired frost having done its purifying work, Pineville emptied itself back into the Santee rice and cotton fields and protracted

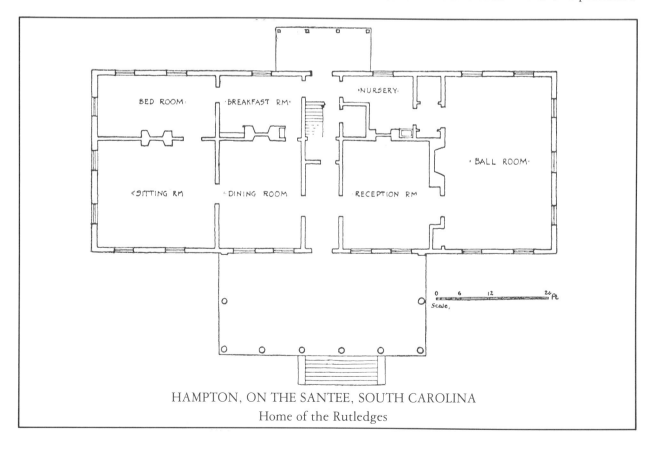

HAMPTON, ON THE SANTEE, SOUTH CAROLINA
Home of the Rutledges

HAMPTON, ON THE SANTEE, SOUTH CAROLINA
Home of the Rutledges

house-parties took the place of the daily coming and going of guests. These balls on the whole were very simple affairs and began early. The lady leading the first set called the figures, and such dear romantic old tunes as "Money Musk," "Haste to the Wedding," and "La Belle Catherine" were popular favorites at Pineville long after they had been forgotten elsewhere. The staple dance of every evening's entertainment was the cotillon. Late in the evening the reel was called and the gayeties were concluded with the boulangèr, "a dance," says a clever writer, "whose quiet movements seem to come in appropriately in order to allow the revellers to cool off before exposing themselves to the night air." The boulangèr, by the way, was the most important dance of the evening, for the partners walked home together by the light of a lantern held by a servant, who hurried on ahead. Fever was the summer epidemic in the Santee swamps, but love and love-making were summer epidemics at Pineville.

The tract of land marked "French Santee" on all the old maps of the Carolinas took its name from the fact that in 1689,[3] or thereabouts, a colony of French Hu-

The Deserted Parlor
HAMPTON, ON THE SANTEE, SOUTH CAROLINA

[3] Some authorities give the date as 1694.

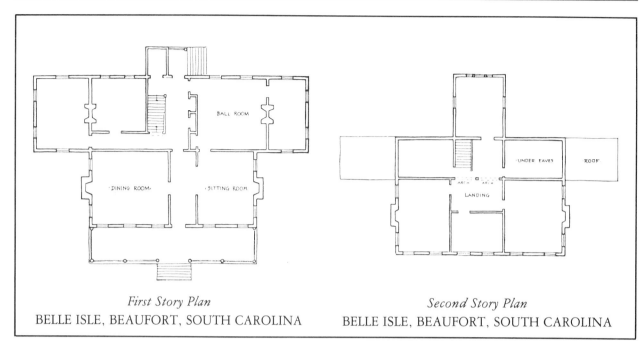

First Story Plan
BELLE ISLE, BEAUFORT, SOUTH CAROLINA

Second Story Plan
BELLE ISLE, BEAUFORT, SOUTH CAROLINA

guenots, in all a hundred and eighty families, driven from France by the Revocation of the Edict of Nantes, settled the High Hills of the Santee and the low lands referred to, which were to be afterwards known as St. James's Parish. Among these immigrants were some bearing names that are well known in South Carolina to this day, such as Huger, Porcher, Ravenel, Legaré, St. Julien, Prioleau, Du Bosc, De Saussure, Laurens, Mazycks, Manigault and many others. Almost all of these French people built their homes on the banks of these to-be-historic waters, some settling in the low delta between the two forks of the river; others migrating farther south to what was afterwards St. Stephen's Parish, or "English Santee," as it was popularly called; and still others pushing as far inland as what is now St. John's Parish.

At the time of the Revolutionary War the Santee River was settled by descendants of the French Huguenots, from French Santee to Eutaw Springs—where General Morgan finally overcame the cruel Tarleton in 1781—most of whom owned savannahs of one size or another and cultivated crops of rice, indigo or cotton.

One of the best known Santee savannahs was The Rocks, which was acquired by Captain Guillard in 1794, and owned by his descendants for generations. White Plains was also well known, as was Milford, the estate of General Moultrie. Wantoot was the savannah of Daniel Ravenel,[4] the son of Réné Ravenel, the first of the name in America. Gravel Hill was a place of considerable celebrity on the Santee, and Belle Isle, the plantation of that illustrious soldier Francis Ma-

rion, though in wretched repair, is still to be seen by the occasional visitor who makes a pilgrimage to it. The place is now owned by one of General Marion's descendants and namesakes. The house is practically deserted and the plantation is not always under cultivation. Though unoccupied and fast falling into ruins, the house is full of quaint old family relics, such as mahogany furniture in excellent designs, old books and old crockery, all left to dust and decay.

The present inhabitants of old French Santee are for the most part the descendants of the original settlers, and their homesteads have come to them through generations. Although the original Huguenots made no effort to preserve their nationality, and their children were allowed to speak English and were encouraged to become loyal adherents to the British crown, there still remain in the domestic life of the region many traces of the origin of the people who inhabit it. The *pillau*, for instance, is even now a common dish on their tables, and that cake called in England a *waffle* is known by them as a *gauffre*. In summertime superfluous fresh meat is still "jerked"; and in French Santee, as elsewhere in South Carolina where the influence of the French Huguenot and his customs have invaded, potted meats still delight the senses with their peculiarly savory odors and delicious flavors. Names, too, are pronounced there with a foreign accent to this day. Thus, Du Bosc is "Du Bŭsk" in French Santee, and Marion "Mahion."

Up to a hundred years ago, the Santee region was well settled and populous. It was connected with Georgetown and Charleston by means of a well-kept stage-road traveled daily by the ponderous vehicles of

---

[4] Daniel Ravenel died in 1807.

BELLE ISLE, BEAUFORT, SOUTH CAROLINA

those times, drawn by four stout horses, and having post-houses and taverns for the refreshment of travelers at intervals along the route. But the old-fashioned stage has also disappeared into the past, and the French Santee is inaccessible to the outside world for a distance of forty miles save by private conveyance. Gone, too, are the inns, and the traveler is now compelled to make his trip through this almost trackless wilderness in a single day, whatever be the weather or condition of his team. Here is heard no shriek of locomotive, no whistle of steamer. No tourist treads its solemn groves of pine, or wanders in delight under the cathedral arches of its mighty oaks.

That portion of Craven County south of the Santee River is marked by a species of solitary grandeur almost unequaled of its kind. Uninterrupted forests of pine and cypress trees stretch off endlessly, with what were once well-worn avenues running through them, and an occasional stately old home looming up in the lonely distance. Now and then a church comes in view, St. Stephen's,[5] for instance which stands so that it can

be seen from afar by those who approach it from the west, or the east, by the main, or river road. This church, like the old homes of those inhabitants who planned it and who once made up the society of French Santee, tells a story of past importance and present desolation. All around it are graves, some of which are quite lost in the fast-encroaching wood; others are enclosed by walls and marked with quaint stones, and overrun with creepers. The stones of many have fallen and those that are still standing are worn by the wind and weather of years. "If you stand on one side of the church," says a writer, recalling his visit to St. Stephen's, "and look through the open doors (and they are never closed), you see a road coming from the south. . . . On the right and on the left the same unbroken line of road appears. In this perfect solitude, whence do they come? Strange and mysterious traces of life and civilization! To what end do they appear to have been constructed? In this perfect solitude, whence do they come, whither do they lead? Strange that at this spot they should unite, and that they all lead to the grave."

What St. Stephen's is to English Santee, St. James's — commonly called "Old Wamboro" Church — is to French Santee. This quaint old Colonial relic, which ranks third in age among the churches of South Carolina, stands close to the old stage-road, not far from the celebrated estate of Mrs. Daniel Horry called Hampton, and about three miles from the Santee Ferry. It is built of bricks brought from England in the reign of Queen Anne and was first opened for worship in 1768. The building is square, massive, and without grace of architecture. It is paved with brick within and furnished with the high-backed pews of the period and almost equally high, narrow benches which serve

[5] Dalcho, in his *Church History of South Carolina*, gives the following account of St. Stephen's Church: The Parish of St. Stephen's was laid out about 1762. The church is one of the handsomest of the county churches of South Carolina, and would be no mean ornament to Charleston. It is built of brick and neatly finished. It stands on the main river road about 12½ miles from the Santee canal. The north and south sides are ornamented with six Doric pilasters and each end with four of the same order. Upon a brick on the south side is inscribed "A. Howard, Sev. 1767," and on another "F. Villepontoux, Sev. 1767," these being the names of the architects. At the east end is a large slashed window and the usual tables of the decalogue and commandments. At the west end is a large gallery, pewed. There are forty-five pews on the ground floor, which is tiled. There is a handsome mahogany pulpit, on the front panel of which are the initials "I. H. S." The ceiling is finished in the same manner as that of St. Michael's Church, Charleston.

Front View
BELLE ISLE, BEAUFORT, SOUTH CAROLINA

Rear View
BELLE ISLE, BEAUFORT, SOUTH CAROLINA

as seats and run around the sides of the pews. It is in excellent repair, though seldom opened for service. Mrs. Rebecca Motte gave a ponderous Bible and prayer-books to this church with her name and "St. James, Santee," stamped in gilt letters on the covers. So large is the Bible that it can scarcely be lifted in one's arms; yet a British soldier conceived the extraordinary idea of carrying it off to England as a trophy, together with the altar service. There, some years after the Revolution, these stolen articles, exposed for sale in a London bookstall, were purchased by a British officer, who had known Mrs. Motte and received kindness from her, and returned to the church, where they are still used whenever it is opened.

Mrs. Rebecca Motte, by the way, was one of the most celebrated colonial heroines of the South, and the mistress of three historic homes. One of these was the Miles Brewton House, of Charleston, which she inherited from her brother's estate, and which was occupied by the British during the Revolution, as their headquarters. Another was Fort Motte, on the Congaree River, which was also seized by the British and defended by a stockade, and which Mrs. Motte fired with her own hands in order to oust them from it and force a Federal victory under Generals Marion and Lee. The third, El Dorado, was a rice plantation on the Santee, where she moved immediately after the Revolution and erected a dwelling on the estate. In this work she was assisted by her son-in-law, Gen. Thomas Pinckney, aide-de-camp to Washington and later one of the early governors of South Carolina. El Dorado, in all its quaint beauty, filled as it was with historic relics, was burned to the ground several years ago. Mrs. Henry Rutledge, a member of the Pinckney and Horry families, a descendant of Rebecca Motte's and formerly a constant visitor at El Dorado, writes the fol-

lowing description of the old place for the *Georgian Period:* —

"El Dorado," she says, "was approached by a broad, straight avenue, guarded on either side by oaks and magnolias. The central part of the house was occupied by a spacious hall and a beautifully proportioned room used as a library or parlor. The ceiling of this room was lofty, the windows and doors equally so. The walls were paneled in cypress and the whole finished by a handsome carved cornice running all around the top of the room. The narrow mantelpiece, of an impossible height, requiring a step-ladder to reach it, was also carved, as was the doorway — befitting the entrance to an old baronial castle — that led into the hall. On either side of this central part were large projecting wings containing bedrooms of the same lofty type. These opened on a wide corridor, on the opposite side of which were many large windows that looked out on the court yard below. These wings were connected by a long, sunny piazza. On the north side of the house was a large porch inlaid with tiles — black and white — and enclosed by an iron balustrade. The roof was supported by massive cypress pillars, which were entirely

Mantelpiece
BLUEFORD, SANTEE RIVER DISTRICT,
SOUTH CAROLINA

FAIRFIELD — 1763 — ON THE SOUTH SANTEE, SOUTH CAROLINA
Now the South Santee Sportsman's Club

concealed by ivy. Ivy and a climbing rose clothed with tender grace the somewhat ruinous double flight of stone steps which led to the grounds below, where was once a labyrinth of evergreens, and winding paths led in and out in a bewildering maze. In these grounds have been found both cannon-balls and grape-shot that have lain there a hundred years."

Fairfield is another South Santee mansion of antiquity. It is now fitted up as the "South Santee Sportsman's Club," and is beautifully situated on a bluff forty feet above the river, of which it commands a wide view, up and down. A walk shaded with evergreens runs at the edge of the bluff for a quarter of a mile. It is an ideal winter home, protected equally from the north and east wind by dense shrubberies on either hand. It was built prior to the Revolution by a member of the Pinckney family and was Tarleton's headquarters while he was in this neighborhood; but it has been so modernized as to leave little trace of its original form, except its tiled roof and stack chimneys. The grove of oaks that lead up to the house is remarkably beautiful, and the trees are very aged. Doubtless, Tarleton rode under them in their vigorous youth.

Situated higher up the river is Hampton, before referred to, the home of the Horrys and Rutledges — a

fine wide-spreading house with lofty pillared portico and a stretch of cultivated ground around it reaching out to the woods beyond. Of it, Mrs. Rutledge[6] writes as follows: —

"The central portion of the house is very old, though no one knows the exact date of its erection, and the cypress steps that lead to the second story are worn by the feet of many generations. These rooms are small and the ceiling low, but this original house of eight rooms was enlarged by Mrs. Daniel Horry immediately after the Revolution, affording a well-proportioned parlor with large bedrooms behind as one wing, and as the other a ballroom of noble dimensions and lofty arched ceiling that runs up to the floor of the attic, there being no intervening rooms on the second story. The flooring of this room is perfectly laid and admirably adapted for dancing. It has many large windows, on the cypress panels between which may be seen the traces of the mirrors and sconces which once hung there. The handsome cornice and mantel are carved, as at El Dorado, but the main feature of the room is the huge fireplace, into which visitors may

[6] Mrs. Rutledge and her husband are the present owners [c1902] of Hampton. No one, therefore, could be better qualified than she to give an account of its many quaint features.

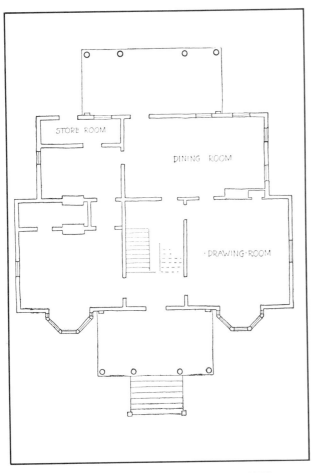

FAIRFIELD, ON THE SOUTH SANTEE, SOUTH CAROLINA

walk at their ease and examine the pictured tiles which line either side. Mrs. Horry and her predecessors understood the comfort and convenience of closets, for there are fifteen in the house, some of them large enough for dressing-rooms, with broad cypress shelves that could furnish better sleeping accommodations than many old-time steamboats. At the back of the house the ground slopes gently to a pretty creek, beyond which rice fields stretch to the river; and this slope is covered with shrubberies, intersected by walks, where birds and squirrels make their happy homes; and in the warm spring days the air is redolent with the perfume of sweet shrubs.

"Hampton claims an honor beyond the other houses in the neighborhood, for General Washington was once its guest. During his Southern tour, in May, 1791, he breakfasted with Mrs. Horry on his way from Georgetown to Charleston. As the sister of his personal friends Gen. Charles Cotesworth Pinckney, who was defeated for the Presidency, in 1800, by John Adams, and Gen. Thomas Pinckney, both of whom were on his personal staff during the Revolution, she

was known to him and he graciously accepted her invitation to break his long ride of fifty miles by a rest at her house. The constant wear of a hundred years has compelled the renewal of most of the front steps by which he entered the house, but two still remain of the original flight. In the cool and spacious ballroom the table was laid, and carefully treasured by Mrs. Horry's descendants may be still seen at Hampton some of the Wedgwood china used on the occasion."

Still another quaint residence of this remote country was Woodville, which has also been destroyed of late by fire.

It was built about 150 years ago—all the materials being imported from England. The family were English, and its appearance reminded one of a keep—without the castle to which it might have belonged. "Imagine," says Mrs. Rutledge, "a circular excavation paved and walled with brick. The earth that was thrown out forms a sloping terrace from the top of the brick wall to the low-lying ground around. This is now overgrown with grass, but removing this and the deep layer of soil on which it grows, the traces of an elevated brick walk, perhaps fifteen feet wide, may be seen encircling the entire moat. In the center of the court yard thus formed stood the turret-like house of four stories—two rooms on a floor. Handsome granite steps bridged the moat back and front, leading to graceful porticos defended with iron railings that give entrance to the second story. The interior of the house was richly decorated with carving and mouldings. The doors, mantels and cornices all were interesting and ornate. The folding shutters are exceedingly curious, and nothing could exceed the quaintness of the tiny attic, full of unexpected corners, weird low cuddy doors, and even here two bedrooms as large as modern doll-houses."

Although the spirit of modern progress has forgotten old "French Santee," nature continues to smile on this quaintly remote region. "In the springtime," says Mrs. Rutledge, "the swamps are unsurpassed in loveliness. The wealth of flowers and variety of exquisite shades of green of the shrubs make it a delight to live out of doors there. The yellow jessamine comes first in point of time, as well as in perfection of beauty, grace and perfume. Then there is the Cherokee rose, climbing with its strong arms to the tops of the tallest trees and drooping thence in immense festoons of glossy dark-green leaves and snowy blossoms. The wistaria abounds on all the water-courses, and the red woodbine and a bush resembling the spirea—a snowy white from top to bottom—grow side by side on the riverbanks. The dogwood gleams ghost-like through the vistas of the forest, the fragile fringe-tree is a dream of grace, and the honeysuckle, in varying shades of white

THE WEDGE, SOUTH SANTEE,
SOUTH CAROLINA

and pink, makes the air faint with perfume, while in the clear streams the iris—true 'fleur-de-lis' of France—grows in profusion. In the sandy soil under the pines are found immense dark-blue violets with stems from four to five inches long. Beds of tiny scented white ones edge the morasses and the banks of the rice fields are carpeted with a prolific light-blue variety."

Until recently this region was a famous hunting ground, for wild turkey, wild duck, woodcock and snipe abounded, and a hundred years ago the old stage regularly transported hampers of game to the city homes of the rice planters of the old "French Santee."

OLD BAPTIST SCHOOLHOUSE, BEAUFORT,
SOUTH CAROLINA

North Front
EL DORADO, ON THE SOUTH SANTEE RIVER, SOUTH CAROLINA

HAMPTON, ON THE SOUTH SANTEE RIVER, SOUTH CAROLINA

Romance and the
South Carolina Homestead

Text by
Olive F. Gunby
Originally published in 1902 as
Volume III of the Georgian Period

Entrance

PARSON'S PLANTATION ON GOOSE CREEK, NEAR CHARLESTON, SOUTH CAROLINA

ROMANCE AND THE SOUTH CAROLINA HOMESTEAD

THE genuine Colonial houses of the South, like the respectable gray-haired servants, are becoming scarce, but certain country-seats dating back to days before this nation had even thought of a housewarming exist yet in South Carolina, secluded in those parishes, close to the sea, where the first colonists got foothold. The young housekeepers in these time-honored dwellings would, doubtless, willingly exchange them for newer quarters less congenial to moths and spiders. Indeed, the old homes owe their preservation as much to the substantial construction that defies fire, and would make the tearing-down a task, as to veneration for their character. But to the person of romantic or antiquarian turn, such a place is eloquent, and merely to cross the plain stone threshold and get a glimpse of the deep-sunk windows and chimney cupboards is to slip back to the time of the minuet and elaborate courtesy, of powdered heads, knee-buckles, buckram skirts and stomachers.

A mansion that interests strangers is Mulberry Castle, on the Cooper River, so-called from the mulberry trees set out for silk culture by an enterprising Governor of the Province. The house bears the date 1714 on the iron vanes which cap its towers. The vanes, of light arabesque design, swing as weathercocks on the four towers and, seen from a distance across the low-lying ricefields, give a quaint mediaeval look to the place. The silk raised and spun on this plantation, the first experimented with in this country, was of fine quality. A patriotic colonial dame carried enough of it for the making of three dresses to prominent women in England in order to demonstrate Carolina's adaptability for silk culture. Mulberry Castle's founder was a zealous churchman who frowned upon dissenters and continued to nip their influence in government affairs.

Many arbitrary, hot-worded arguments bearing on state and martial matters were contested in this old house, and significant negotiations conducted when delegations or private parties sailed up the Cooper to the Castle's master, to have rights vindicated or wrongs redressed. The loopholes provided in the heavy window shutters evidence a martial history. The owner promoted the building of forts as well as churches, and his descendants later experienced rough handling both from Indians and British scouts. Once, in Revolutionary times, a servant reported that troopers were coming across the open hilltop in front of the house. The proprietor—a colonel of the day—went down the slope back of the premises to a schooner anchored in the river, and lying face downward on the deck was covered with a rowboat, in time to hear the troopers gallop past toward the swamp where they believed him hiding.

At another time, while the family was at supper, word came of the enemy's approach. The women promptly blew out the candles, and the husband and father reached his stable and on horseback got off to the woods while the raiders were searching the premises by torchlight. Many colonists were in the house at that juncture because of its supposed safety. On a pallet in one corner of the parlor the master's little daughter had been put to sleep while some visitor occupied her bed. Her couch was overturned by bayonets in the soldiers' search for arms or treasure. Those times gave way to seasons of great prosperity and affluence, and even in the Civil War the Castle escaped damage because of its secluded location.

Two miles from Mulberry plantation is a quaint dwelling called Exeter House, with the date 1712 graved on its brickwork. The two houses are companions, hav-

MULBERRY CASTLE, ON THE COOPER RIVER, SOUTH CAROLINA

ing shared the same history, and being at present owned by family connections.

Drayton Hall, on the Ashley River, is a survival of first settlement days, still habitable after long use and many changes in its surroundings. And Middleton Place, its close neighbor, is possibly the best known of Carolina plantations, famed for its noble gardens, to which hundreds of tourists make pilgrimage. It is there that one sees the clustering azaleas blooming full and free in the open air at the foot of lofty oaks and laurels, from which the gray moss veilings droop almost to the ground. Nowhere else in the country have such effects in blossoms and foliage been contrived, and the charm of the place is its naturalness and freedom from artificial posing. Wherever and whenever the gardener's art has been used to aid nature it has been done so deftly and subtly as to give the impression that even Madam Nature herself had been deceived into mothering the innovation. This estate marks the time when Carolinians first became ambitious for luxury. The founder's aim was to make a choice and cultivated display of the native botanical riches of the section, mingling them with such foreign importations as could best be naturalized to the soil. The very spirit of tranquil loveliness broods over the spot, and even the prosaic visitor warms to enthusiasm at the first surprise of these riverside grounds that many liken to Paradise. The house, to which the gardens were a complement, was burned years ago, but its loss has been skillfully concealed.

In St. James's Parish, Goose Creek, is Yeaman's Hall, whose founder was the first person to introduce slave-labor in Carolina. The house was in constant use until the earthquake cracked its walls. Its age shows in its face. Portholes in the basement brickwork and staircase landing show it to have been designed for defense as well as comfort. And the builder, who fled from Barbadoes, bringing money and slaves with him, must have profited by his lessons in danger, for he not only caused a secret chamber to be walled within the house,

but also built an underground passage leading out, several hundred yards, to the creek, where boats were kept moored that the besieged might leave the dwelling secretly. This passage opens into the family graveyard with adjoins the premises, as was old-country custom. A flat gravestone inscribed to some mythical ancestor hides the entrance to the underground way. That buried passage has been an abiding terror to successive generations of the neighborhood darkies, and been speculated upon by many installments of Sunday-school children who go to the Hall for their spring picnics. The hidden way is the basis for all manner of "bogey stories," and the most harmless of Jacko'-my-Lanterns seen there causes desertion of the territory for weeks, and then the foxes and 'possums roam secure from hunting. A fine spring of water is hard by, but none of the negro tenants on the land partake of its benefit. They say the place is haunted.

There is a ghost story concerning the experience of a governess, a gay young widow, who taught the children of the household some generations after its founding. She was reading a novel one night in her bedchamber upstairs when the door opened softly, and an old lady in silk gown and cross 'kerchief walked in and looked at her, with finger uplifted. The young woman asked the visitor's meaning without getting response, and when the apparition turned to go she followed through several rooms until it vanished as suddenly as it had come. The household was roused and inquiry made as to how a stranger could have got in or out without notice. The mystery was never cleared. Only those familiar with the family characteristics set it down as a warning from a strong-minded grandame of strict religious bent, who, during her sway as mistress, had forbidden all levity and pernicious reading to her household. The private diaries of the time report that the governess destroyed her novel and took a servant-maid to sleep in her room thereafter; but, later, when there arrived at the Hall a son of the old grandame whose features strikingly resembled his mother's, the young woman was thrown into such agitation of mind that she had to go away in quest of health.

An ancient place facing on Wappoo Creek is notable for having produced the first Carolina indigo, an achievement due to woman's wit and perseverance. The Governor of Antigua sent his wife and daughter to his Carolina plantation for the advantages of climate. The daughter, wearying of the monotony of country life, sought for some industry with which to liven matters, and began experimenting with tropical seeds and fruits sent her by her father. The first indigo seeds she planted were killed by frost; the next venture failed because of worms. The third trial after many

Fireplaces
MULBERRY CASTLE, ON THE COOPER RIVER, SOUTH CAROLINA

months proved successful, and the father being advised of the fact sent a West Indian chemist to build vats and show the process of extracting the dye from the weed. The foreign chemist, probably regretting his bargain as adverse to his own country, purposely misled his employer and marred the quality of the indigo by putting in too much lime.

The young woman circumvented him, however. Feeling intuitively that his dealings were not fair, she watched him carefully, questioning every step in the process and his reasons for doing thus and so, with the result that a knowledge of the correct management was obtained and the successful manipulation of indigo made known to the planters of the section. Afterwards, this girl experimenter married a neighbor, to whom her father made a present of all the indigo raised on his lands.

One of the stateliest of the old plantation houses in the low country was Archdale, built in 1706, under the direction of the architect who built St. Philip's Church in Charleston. This house, which had the massive walls of a fortress, with steps and porches to correspond, was injured by the earthquake, which proved so ruinous to brick houses. The interior is decorated with florid stucco-work and the hall fireplaces are lined with pictured Dutch tiles. As in most old English dwellings, the family allegiance is shown by the royal arms, done in stucco, over the main archway. Without were paved courts and extensive grounds adorned with laurel and catalpa trees and flowering shrubs.

Some of these old places stand far back from the road and owe much of their beauty to a water approach or to their isolation among live-oak groves, or on imposing bluffs visible from some distance. Bits of social or domestic history are connected with each, serving to fix them in memory. You drive up some avenue so well defined and stately it would seem the caretaker must be near at hand, only to find the relics of a dwelling and grounds long defaced, the well-filled barns at a little distance and the populous negro cabins emphasizing the desolation. One such home near Charleston was destroyed by its owner's hand on discovery that the enemy was approaching. His negroes strove to prevent the sacrifice, but Spartan-like, the planter himself, believing that the place would be sacked, applied the torch that took away valuable paintings, plate and household keepsakes. At another old home-site in a sister parish, the tale holds of the young master's journeying across the ocean for his bride, after building a carefully planned house with express deference to her comfort. The night of the homecoming the carriage was sent to the station to fetch the young pair, and as they entered the avenue leading to the house an odd light struck on the trees. The dwelling was on fire, too far gone to be rescued. And the couple sat in their conveyance and watched the tragedy, afterwards taking shelter in the overseer's house until a substitute could be built.

There are no older or more picturesque survivals anywhere in the land than these Carolina home-sites; and it is well to record them before they have been too much modified or set aside.

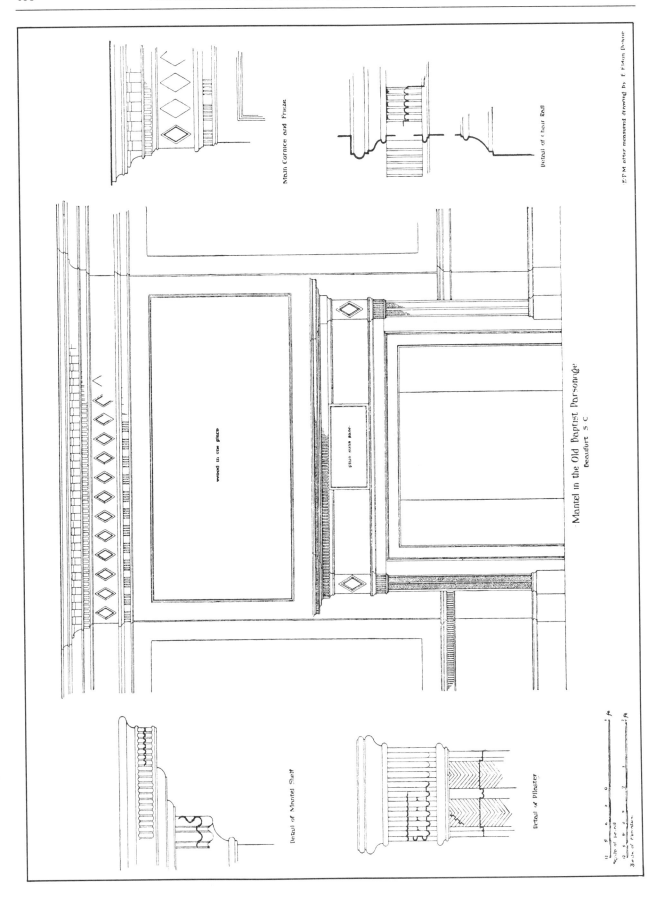

Main Cornice and Frieze

Detail of Chair Rail

Mantel in the Old Baptist Parsonage
Beaufort S C

Detail of Mantel Shelf

Detail of Pilaster

E.T.M. after measured drawing by F. Eldon Deane

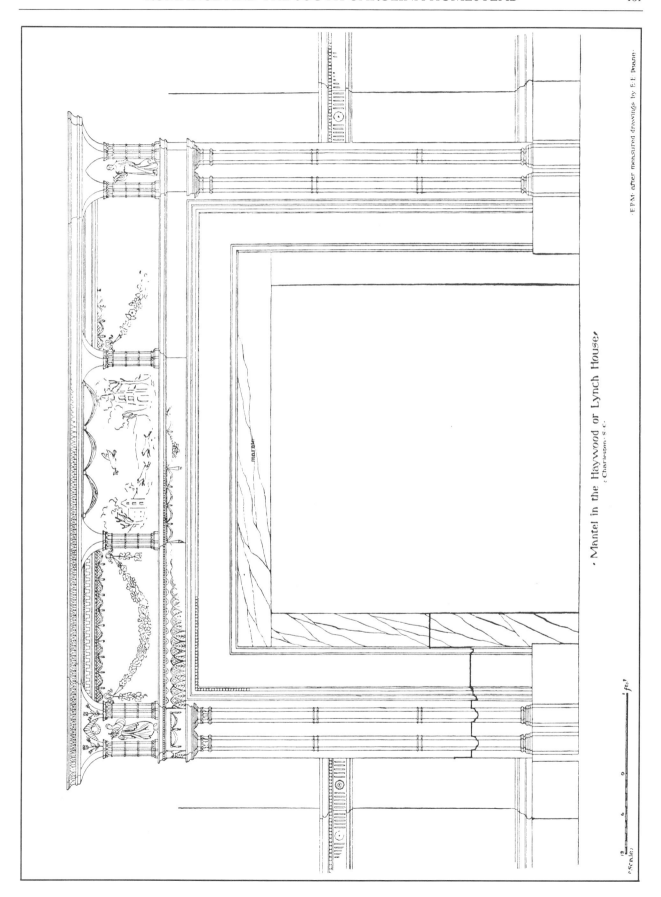

Mantel in the Haywood or Lynch House,
Charleston, S.C.

The Pickets
BULL PLANTATION, ASHLEY RIVER, SOUTH CAROLINA

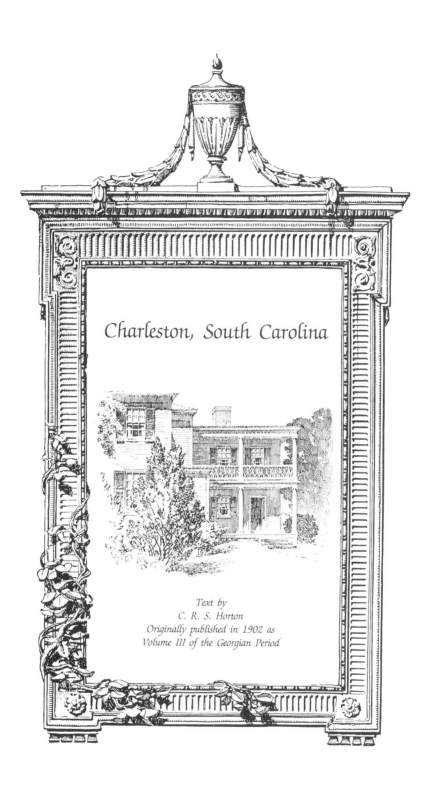

Charleston, South Carolina

Text by
C. R. S. Horton
Originally published in 1902 as
Volume III of the Georgian Period

HORRY HOUSE, CORNER MEETING AND TRADD STREETS, CHARLESTON, SOUTH CAROLINA

CHARLESTON, BETWEEN ASHLEY AND COOPER

THE Charleston[1] we know today presents, architecturally, a quaint mixture of French and English ideas, together with some of the more salient ones of old San Domingo, in the way of exaggerated verandas and high brick walls, thrown in for good measure. The first two of these *motifs*—the French and the English—were inherited, naturally enough, from its earliest inhabitants, the English Cavalier and the French Huguenot, both of whom represented people of pronounced opinions as to what constituted domestic comfort and elegance. The San Domingo feeling came naturally and regularly enough, too, along with a lot of wealthy immigrants from the West Indian Islands who made their homes in Charleston, where the climate was not totally unlike that left behind them, and proceeded to make themselves comfortable in their own way.

The houses built by these immigrants were usually spacious, with enormous two and three story covered verandas as special features, though quite lacking in interior adornment. They were commonly surrounded by large grounds around which high brick walls were built, after the manner of that surrounding the Simonton residence[2] on Légare Street, which, with its

great iron gateway, is one of the showplaces of the city. These walls afforded the greatest privacy—a thing always of paramount importance with Charlestonians—and allowed the outsider no glimpse of the well-arranged garden within with its gay masses of odorous opoponax, *rêve d'or* roses and tropical palmetto bushes, among which the women of the family wandered informally at pleasure—or, if any, just a tantalizing peep through the richly wrought entrance

Although these San Domingo houses had no feeling of Classicism, toward which the Cavaliers and their descendants, being men of culture and wide social experience, were greatly inclined, they were so practical and comfortable, so thoroughly adapted to the demands of the climate and the hospitable life of the South, and so much less expensive, on the whole, than Georgian houses of the type of the Miles Brewton House, built in 1765, and the Lord William Campbell House on Meeting Street, that, little by little, the style became almost universal among the masses as well as the classes. So much so that, modified, amplified, and beautified by French or English ideas of adornment, it became in due time—high walls, great gateways, and all—what might accurately be called the Charleston type, and continued its vogue—despite the seductive influence of the Greek Revival, which began to make its influence felt at the beginning of the nineteenth century—until the Civil War.

These typical houses were situated in two different manners, the more popular of which was to turn an end of the house to the street, running it up on a line with the sidewalk, leaving a seemingly endless expanse of veranda to open on a side garden. A perfect illustration of this method of locating a residence is afforded by the George Edmondson House on Légare Street, now owned by Capt. J. Adger Smythe. Here the dwelling itself presents on first sight the average ap-

---

[1] CHARLESTON—Charleston was settled in 1680 by English colonists under Col. William Sayle, and called New Charles Town because of abortive attempts to found earlier cities of the same name in the same general locality as far back as 1670. Its geographical position is similar to that of Manhattan Island in that it is bounded on either side by rivers of considerable width—the Cooper to the east and the Ashley to the west—and faces the harbor to the southeast.

[2] SIMONTON—The Simonton residence was built some time between 1740 and 1770, and at that time, as the original plan shows, the garden attached to the premises was laid out. The wall was built by a silk merchant, Lorentz, who purchased the property toward the end of the eighteenth century. The gate was a somewhat later structure, and is said to have been the work of a German, by the name of Werner, who was a genius in ironwork.

Entrance

BULL HOUSE, BULL STREET, CHARLESTON, SOUTH CAROLINA

pearance of a town house, with a simple but well designed entrance from the street. By peering about
carefully, however, through the vines and trees and
seeking the proper position for a good view, the formal front, or *side*, to speak more properly, is found to
be but a mask for a characteristically Southern mansion of extraordinary size, surrounded by an extensive
garden shut off from the street by a high wall of brick,
wood and iron, the feature of which is a remarkably
fine gateway[3] which, in connection with the grilled
entrance, forms a continuous design. This doorway,
by the way, does not lead into the house proper, as
one might imagine, but — after the manner of most
Charleston doorways — up several steps on the inside to

the first floor of the veranda, the existence of which a
stranger passing by the apparent front would not
suspect.

The other "manner" referred to placed the house in
the midst of large grounds some distance from the
street. Although here again it was sometimes turned
endwise, it was more generally given a full front to the
thoroughfare, as in the case of the De Saussure House
on South Battery. As a rule, too, they were built after
the general plan of this house — three stories high,
with a three-story columned veranda stretching across
the entire front upon which the full-length windows
of the rooms open. From the house a wide sandy walk
leads down to the carriage gate, flanked on one side by
a smaller gate where the family enters and where visitors pause to ring a bell, and on the other by the
servants' entrance.

The interior arrangement of these huge old San
Domingo houses is exceedingly simple, consisting, as a
rule, of a central hall, with one great room on either
side of it supplied with long windows to catch the
breeze. Having only two rooms to a floor with an occa-

---

[3] The Edmondson gateway has served as a model for many others
in Charleston and elsewhere, none of which, however, equal the
original in beauty. The wrought iron work was imported from England with the initials of the builder as features of the grillework on
either side of the doorway. The fashion of introducing such initials
in wrought iron trimmings prevailed in Charleston, an example of
which is also furnished by the entrance to the Nathaniel Russell
house on Meeting Street, which was built about 1790, and also by
the veranda railing of an old antiquities shop on Queen Street.

Gateway
EAST BATTERY, CHARLESTON, SOUTH CAROLINA

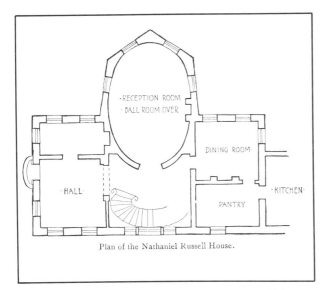

Plan of the Nathaniel Russell House.

NATHANIEL RUSSELL HOUSE, CHARLESTON

sional one or two story L to the rear and the servants' quarters in an addition to the right or left (see quarters to De Saussure House on page 126) it became necessary to add numerous stories to the original one in order to secure the number of apartments needed for the accommodation of an average-size family. The pushing of these houses upward instead of spreading them outward over a larger area, while it added to their coolness—a thing most to be desired in a hot climate—certainly produced very *outré* and remarkable effects; which, on the whole, however, are unique though ungainly, and sometimes positively baronial and a trifle *awful*, as in the case of the Holmes House on East Battery, which, though slightly different in form, illustrates the same idea of construction and in which the style may be said to have reached its extremest limit. This house was built by James Gadsden Holmes, Sr., in 1818, and was until long after the war (during which, being white and the highest building on the Battery, it was used for target practice by the Federals and frequently hit) the residence of his family, by members of which it is still owned. For years, however, it has been practically deserted while seeking a purchaser. The great rooms are bare except for stray bits of old mahogany furniture, most of the wood of which, by the way, came from San Domingo. In the dusty, webby old arched dining room, for instance, stands an antique sideboard of simple design but good wood and excellent workmanship, with its doors aimlessly open—left behind as a thing of no value. A curious old desk is in the hall with a leaded glass case above for books and three large drawers below, the top one of which lets down to form a writing shelf. In the octagon drawing room above the arched entrance several old family portraits lean wearily against the wall—two by

Copley and one by Flagg; and in the attic, up five long flights of stairs, half concealed by a lot of old *Edinburgh Reviews* of 1812–1814 and other dilapidated books which speak plainly of the cultured tastes of those who once inhabited the rooms below, lies an old satinwood four poster, one standard of which has poked itself through the open door of an attic wine closet there.

Attic wine closets, by the way, are among the many unique features of the homes of the rich in old Charleston. In them the madeiras for which the city was so famous were stored, as the action of the sun on the roof produced a higher temperature than could have been obtained in a subterranean closet and the slight motion of the house was considered desirable during fermentation.

According to the earliest records, madeira was the common drink in Charleston in 1763. In the middle of the eighteenth century it became fashionable in England owing to the recommendation of officers who had served in the West Indies and America. It became customary to ship the wine from Madeira to the West Indies and thence to America to improve its taste. This journeying, in a measure, took the place of submitting the wines to a high temperature in stone buildings. The early shippers found that the climate of Charleston was especially adapted to mellowing the wine and imparting to it that peculiar bouquet and flavor so prized by connoisseurs and stored large quantities of it there. So famous, in fact, was the wine of old Charleston that the British Consul was instructed to purchase wine for the Queen's table there and annually did so, selecting it from the cellars of private gentlemen. Much fine old wine is still stored in the cellars of the rich and aristocratic families of Charleston, though it is rapidly disappearing. The oldest wine known there now is in the possession of the Blake family and is 146 years old. The Blake wine is known historically as the "Earthquake wine," having been brought to Charleston the year of the great Lisbon earthquake, 1755. Dr. Gabriel Manigault had, prior to his death, a few dozen bottles of the celebrated "Belvedere," named from the vessel that brought it from Madeira in 1838. There is still a quantity of the famous "Jockey Club" madeira in Charleston held, under a perhaps mistaken faith in its keeping qualities, at exorbitant prices. It is so called because at the Jockey Club balls, instituted more than a century ago, it was the brand served.

From the roof of the Holmes House one may enjoy a perfect view of the city of Charleston, from the green fertile islands lying beyond the harbor to the south, far up the Ashley and Cooper rivers to the north, with the Wrenesque spire of St. Michael's standing up white and clear against the vivid blue of the sky—less deli-

Doorway
NATHANIEL RUSSELL HOUSE, CHARLESTON, SOUTH CAROLINA

cate in outline, however, than the more recent spire of St. Philip's, not far away.

The oldest part of the city of Charleston, as laid out by John Culpepper in 1680 and presented for the first time in a map drawn by Edward Crisp in 1704, extended from the sea on the south to what was formerly a creek on the north, where the celebrated Charleston market now stands, which was established as early as 1788, although the present market house was not built until 1841. On the east it was bounded by Cooper River and extended west as far as Meeting Street, at the extreme limit of which stood what was then a public market, with St. Philip's Church—which was the first English church in South Carolina—on the site where St. Michael's now stands. From this point, which may now be pointed out as the corner of Meeting and Broad streets, to the Battery, streets intersected each other, consisting of eight in all and one alley, namely: Tradd Street, Elliot Street, Broad and Queen streets

running east and west; and Bay, Union (now State), Church and Meeting streets running north and south.

Tradd Street, a quaint, narrow, silent thoroughfare paved with cobblestones, is today one of the most interesting sights afforded the student of Coloniana visiting Charleston. A plain old house that formerly stood at the corner of Tradd and East Bay was the residence of Robert Tradd, from whom the street took its name and in which the first native child was born. Not far away, on the southwest corner of East Bay and Longitude Lane, the pretentious dwelling of Landgrave Thomas Smith used to stand, on a lot in the rear of which the first rice in South Carolina is believed to have been planted as far back as 1693. On the north side of Tradd Street, about midway between Church and East Bay streets, the old Carolina Coffeehouse still stands. In its day this was the leading fashionable hotel in the city. The Governor and his staff lodged there and it was the scene of all the public dinners

NATHANIEL RUSSELL HOUSE, CHARLESTON

Doorway
NATHANIEL RUSSELL HOUSE, CHARLESTON, SOUTH CAROLINA

· Janitor's Entrance Lodge · Charleston College ·
· Charleston · S·C ·
[1785]

given to strangers. Tradd Street, in the old days, was a social thoroughfare. Church Street, at right-angles, not far away, was equally so.

Any one interested in the architectural characteristics of Charleston should enter this historic roadway at the Battery, from which it takes its narrow and winding course past old iron gateways and high brick walls, overgrown with cypress vine and Virginia creeper; under the projecting hoods of doorways, toward the heart of the city, crossing at intervals streets equally quaint and curious. Looking down Longitude Lane and St. Michael's Alley one could almost imagine one's self in old Havana, while down Tradd or Queen Street, toward East Bay, there are futures that suggest the French Quarter of New Orleans.

East Bay Street itself, with its wharves, storehouses and dilapidated old dwellings, now turned into tenements and fast going to ruin, many of them being already wholly uninhabitable, is curiously unlike any modern street in any modern town, although, at one time, it was a favorite residence section of the rich, fronting, as it does, toward both Cooper River and the sea. One of the notable houses of this vicinity stands on the corner of Laurens and East Bay streets, sur-

rounded by the remains of what was once a garden, part of which is now used as a city dumping-ground. This house, which was formerly bare of its present verandas, was built about 1770 by Henry Laurens, the first President of the Continental Congress, Minister Plenipotentiary to Holland, a friend of Washington's, and one of our most picturesque national characters. Just across the street from it is Heyward House, one of the many in Charleston built by members of that distinguished family, another of which is just a stone's throw away, at 87 Church Street.[4] With its great old gateway and Corinthian portico it is not easily overlooked or forgotten, for it possesses, more than most

_____

[4] HEYWARD HOUSE—The Heyward House referred to on Church Street is now [c1900] used as a bakery and is situated near the corner of Tradd. It was the residence of Judge Thomas Heyward, a signer of the Declaration of Independence and a friend of George Washington's, who on his Southern tour, in 1791, was a guest in this house. At that time it was one of the most splendid residences in the city. A double-story veranda jutted out over the street, said to have been similar in general style to that of the Horry House, corner of Meeting and Tradd, and the interior furnishing was second to none in the city. The drawing room on the second floor is a fine chamber containing some interesting features still in excellent preservation.

THE COLLEGE OF CHARLESTON, SOUTH CAROLINA

Charleston houses, a peculiar and persistent *genius* of its own. The interior is almost equally interesting. The paneled drawing room on the second floor, overlooking the river, is a charming chamber with an atmosphere of nobler days; and many of the mantels throughout the house, though greatly mutilated by tenement renters, are excellent specimens, worthy of preservation. Not far away is the old Ball residence, and others equally valuable as specimens of brickwork and woodwork, and often containing superb old staircases,[5] not so remarkable for their adornment (Charleston staircases being almost invariably of plain mahogany, devoid of carving) as for their masterly construction. Here also may be found an interesting

[5] THE ELLIOT STAIRCASE — One of the finest staircases in the entire city is that of the old Elliot residence, which was built before the Revolution, and is now [c1900] the offices of the Charleston Waterworks. This stairway of solid marble goes from basement to attic, and without a support, except on the side towards the wall. The upper story is one large room covering the entire building, except the hall, and was built for a ballroom. The view from the window looking seaward is as fine as there is in the city. On the side of the main stairway is a private, or secret, stairway, built in the solid masonry, with an opening on each floor. Servants in showing a guest would conduct him to the foot of the main stairway and, directing him up, would meet him at the landing on the next floor, and so on to the upper story, or ballroom. No servant was allowed to go up the main stairway with company.

display of wrought iron railings, window screens, brackets and other trimmings — in which, by the way, Charleston is particularly rich as a city — some of the designs of which are charmingly simple, others being highly elaborate and worthy to rank with the best work of Queen Anne's reign. Much of the simpler work in wrought iron — which, on the whole, is more valuable than that which is more elaborate, in that it is more original — is said to have been the work of an old blind slave, who at one time followed the blacksmith's calling in Charleston.

The residences of old Charleston which are still preserved are, for the most part, quite plain externally, and of rather forbidding mien. High walls enclose their court yards, over the tops of which the antique slave quarters — which with their red-tiled roofs are a touch of old Spain in the general scheme of construction — are still to be seen. The dwelling and quarters are usually of brick, the former being often roughcast. Occasionally, however, they were of black cypress, as in the case of the old Drayton House, on South Battery, which, with its richly adorned interior, is one of the choicest Colonial specimens in the city.

The oldest English houses in Charleston, although most of them are now supplied with verandas, which

LOWNDES (WAGGONER) HOUSE,

were found to be necessary because of the climate, were originally built without them, and were entered from the street on the ground floor, as in the case of Mrs. William Mason-Smith's house on Church Street; or, at most, up a high stoop, as in the Lord William Campbell House on Meeting Street, or Hayne House, just across the way from it. The Mason-Smith House has long verandas, not to be seen from the immediate front, running along the entire side of the house, upon which the full-length windows of the different rooms open. These verandas immediately overlook the adjacent churchyard with its quaint gravestones, some of which seem to be bending their necks and standing on tip-toe to peep through the windows into the cherry rooms just beyond the dividing-wall. The draw-

ing room of this house is a long double chamber on the second floor, the two mantels of which are not unlike the one in the drawing room of Brewton House, and the woodwork throughout is exceedingly refined and quite elaborate.

Second-story drawing rooms, by the way, are the rule and not the exception in Charleston, which holds with great tenacity to its English ideas of social life, in connection with which a great deal more of formality obtains than in any other Southern city; and the line between social and business intercourse is very closely drawn. And such quaint Old World formality! A caller entering any of the old Charleston houses is first given a seat in the hall—which, as a rule, is cheerless and unattractive—while his card is presented. If his

CHARLESTON, SOUTH CAROLINA

mission is a business one, or he is paying a visit to a masculine member of the household, he is asked into the library, which is usually the first room on the first floor looking out directly on the street. If, however, he is to be the guest of the ladies, the servant, returning, shows him, with a great flourish of politeness and ceremony, upstairs into the drawing room, which, in even the least pretentious of the old houses, is the long chamber occupying the front section of the second story and may be either a stately audience-chamber with vaulted ceiling and a rich display of woodwork — as in the case of the Miles Brewton House before referred to — or a quaint low chamber with chair boards, the freize and ceiling of the room being elaborately adorned with delicate patterns in plaster or putty after the style introduced by the Brothers Adam about 1760, which was popular in Charleston.[6] Often the walls were wainscoted all the way, and invariably the main feature of the room is a fine old mantel carried up to the ceiling.

The antique mahogany with which these rooms are furnished presents a study in bygone fashions both interesting and valuable, and the walls are hung with portraits by Copley, Flagg, Savage, Sully, Peale, Trumbull, Gilbert, and many other colonial painters not so well known, men who, by the way, are deservedly obscure; with miniatures by Washington Allston,

[6] Some of this mural decoration is said to have been imported from Italy and by skilled hands has been attached to the wall in set designs by means of brass tacks that are adroitly concealed.

HENRY LAURENS HOUSE, LAURENS AND EAST BAY STREETS, CHARLESTON

Malbone and Fraser, and an occasional St. Mémin engraving to lend quaint interest and completeness to the art collection. Nowhere in America have the families inherited for generations so many valuable *objets d' art,* which, to their credit be it said, they have appreciated and clung to through all changes of fortune. No one can but wonder after visiting at different classes of homes, all of which were stocked with old mahogany and hung with quaint portraits of different grades of excellence, where the antiquities dealers secure their wares. None of the families seem to have sold any of their possessions for generations. And yet if, on your way up Church Street past the little Gothic Huguenot temple, built in 1841 on the site where a Huguenot church has stood since 1692, to where the portico of old St. Philip's looms before you in solemn dignity and beauty, you chance to stop in for a moment at one of the antiquities shops, you will see wonderful old four posters, carved in the celebrated pineapple pattern, or with wheat sheaves, or roses, or what not; quaint wine-coolers and tidy, light sideboards, with inlaid trimmings and medallions in lighter wood, that the dealer will tell you are real Chippendales — regardless of the fact that Chippendale's work was usually massive, and he is said not to have used inlay —; and elaborately carved chairs which, unless you chance

to know the difference, he will convince you are real Sheratons going at a sacrifice.

By far the richest storehouse of old furniture, ceramics and art in Charleston, as well as the finest piece of Georgian architecture in South Carolina, is Brewton House commonly spoken of there as the Bull-Pringle House, which surpasses all of its contemporaries in architectural merit and enrichment. It was built in 1760 by Miles Brewton,[7] a wealthy Charleston merchant, the plans and most of the woodwork being

---

[7] Miles Brewton, after enjoying the comforts of his new home for a few years only, was, together with his entire family, lost at sea and his property inherited by his three sisters. One of these, Mrs. Rebecca Brewton Motte, the celebrated Revolutionary heroine, was living in the house during the Revolution, when it was seized by Sir Henry Clinton for his headquarters and later turned over by him to Lord Rawdon. Its occupancy by the British saved it from destruction during this period when so many Charleston houses were burned and sacked. It was again the headquarters of the enemy during the Civil War, and again saved from destruction though considerably damaged. Mrs. Motte is associated not only with the history of this place, but with that of two others, also celebrated. One of these was her home on the Congaree (to which she retired when Brewton House was taken from her), which was shortly after seized by the British and called Fort Motte, and which she herself fired to force them to evacuate. The other was a romantic old mansion built by her on her rice plantation on South Santee called El Dorado, which was burned a few years ago.

One of Mrs. Motte's daughters married Mr. William Allston, whose youngest daughter married William Bull-Pringle.

JUDGE THOMAS HEYWARD'S HOUSE,
CHURCH STREET, CHARLESTON

imported from England. Although later in date than Shirley, on the James River, and even than Drayton Hall, on the Ashley, which was built in 1742, like these earlier houses, it is a notable example of the two-story porch treatment in Colonial work; and though a town residence and not a manor house, as in the other two instances, it is no less a mecca to which students of Colonial work come for inspiration. It fronts on lower King Street, with a forecourt enclosed by a brick wall, 15 feet high, flanking on either side a wrought iron fence in the immediate front, which, though lower than the wall, is rendered even less scalable by a finish of feudal spikes pointing in every direction.

Entering through the fine old doorway, centrally placed, the architrave of which is supported by pilasters, one finds himself in a stone-flagged hall, running through to the rear and dividing the lower floor into two suites, which might be termed the dining and library suites, all the doorways leading into which have rich entablatures. The two halls—front and rear—the dado of both of which is of dark mahogany, paneled, are separated by the usual flat archway supported by detached columns of a Doric order, the cornice of which is the same throughout. Facing you from the end of the rear hall is a handsome mahogany staircase of two flights, with gracefully turned banisters and carved stair-ends and a half-pace landing at the end of the first flight. The feature of this landing is a deeply recessed three-light window which affords ample illumination to both the upper and lower passages in even the dullest weather. From this landing one has an excellent view of the quaint old court yard in the rear with its set flowerbeds and wilderness of fine old shrubs; and its even quainter slave quarters, the ga-

bled end of which suggests, curiously enough, a Gothic temple.

The upper hall of the Brewton House is of very dignified and elaborate character, with its heavily pedimented doors to the different chambers, and its deeply arched entrance to the drawing room, which, by the way, has been pronounced by critics the most beautiful Colonial room in America. This drawing room is a long, most lovely chamber, with its rich dado, lofty paneled walls, handsome cornice, and coved ceiling; with its mantel carried up to the ceiling, from the remote center of which hangs the most elaborately handsome crystal chandelier to be found in any of our Colonial houses. A peculiarity of this chandelier is that the tall glass candleshades, intended to protect the burning taper from any breeze that might be afloat, are still perfectly preserved and occasionally allowed to perform their function, as on a recent occasion, when a reception was given in their ancestral house by the Misses Pringle in honor of the social début of one of their young relatives.

The drawing room occupies the full width of the room below, including that of the hall, also, and is lighted by five windows. Three of these overlook King Street and face you on entering. The other two are on the south side of the chamber and between them hangs a French mirror of great age. Aside from its architectural value this room could not fail to interest even a casual observer in that it is a veritable museum, the contents of which have not been collected from a hundred shops, but, handed down, have been en-

Tombs (1805)
PRINCE GEORGE'S CHURCHYARD,
GEORGETOWN, SOUTH CAROLINA

Tombstone of Mrs. Benj. Elliott (1767)
ST. PHILIP'S CHURCHYARD, CHARLESTON,
SOUTH CAROLINA

riched by each generation of an old and cultured family. Not the least important of the many valuable features of this museum are the portraits. Over the mantel hangs a Sully—one of his best—the subject being the grandmother of the present owners of the house. Occupying the place of honor, between the mantel and the entrance, is a full-length portrait of Mrs. William Allston, *née* Motte—their grandmother—in her brocaded paniers and powdered hair. This portrait was executed in 1793 by E. Savage, who spent considerable time in the United States making studies, which he finished at his leisure. Not far away is a portrait of Miles Brewton himself, done by Sir Joshua Reynolds in 1756; and on the mantel, among a collection of valuable miniatures, is one of John Julius Pringle, done by Charles Fraser, who ranks with Allston and Malbone as the best of our American miniaturists.

In an article on the "Customs of Old Charleston," William G. Whilden writes of the furniture commonly used as follows:—

"In the corner as you entered the door in the dining-room stood the 'wine-cooler,' of polished mahogany, inlaid with wreaths of satinwood; octagon in shape; about three feet high, on six spindling square legs; divided inside with compartments, each to hold a bottle of wine; the centre lined with lead to hold ice or water. Being on rollers, it was wheeled up to the side of the host at the head of the table and the cooled bottles handed out as needed.

"The sideboard, with its large, deep drawers, six in number, and three closets, was large enough to con-

tain all that could be put into three or four of the more fashionable kind now in use. On each side, like sentinels, stood the sloping-top knife, fork and spoon cases lined with green baize; alongside of each stood the silver bottle-stands containing cut-glass decanters; and in the centre the goblet and tumblers for daily use.

"On the mantelpiece, in the centre, was the snuffers and tray. On the end of the mantelpiece was to be found the tinder-box and flint and steel, and possibly a few slips of lightwood, the end of which had been dipped in brimstone, the more easily to obtain a light if a stray spark went into the tinder-box. The mantelpiece itself was so high that no child could reach it without mounting on a chair, and the fireplace large enough to hold what would now be a day's supply of wood. In the corner stood the old clock with its long pendulum, showing, besides the time, the day of the month, the condition of the moon, the rising of the tide and of the sun, with 'Made by John Carmichael, Glasgow, Scotland,' across its face."

At the time Brewton House was at the height of its pristine splendor, Izard House, just across on Meeting Street (not a stone's throw away), was another scene of high social life. This interesting old residence, of English brick, is now looked upon as a Colonial landmark and is pointed out as the residence of one of the Royal Governors. And so it was, its official occupant being Lord William Campbell, whose wife, *née* Izard, inherited the house from her father. And from it Lord and Lady Campbell escaped by way of a creek, that then

Tombstone (1789)
ST. PHILIP'S CHURCHYARD, CHARLESTON,
SOUTH CAROLINA

Entrance
HAYNE HOUSE, MEETING STREET, CHARLESTON

flowed at the rear of their house where Water Street now runs, to an English man-of-war in the harbor.

The Izard House, or to speak more popularly, the Lord William Campbell House, although quite dissimilar in external design from Brewton House, is not unlike it in its general interior plan, having a very similar staircase leading to the second-story hall, at the front of which sweeps a long drawing room, the ceiling of which is decorated with an elaborate design executed in putty.

Across the street from the Lord Campbell House is Hayne House, said to have been the pre-Revolutionary abode of the martyr Hayne; but a close examination of records refutes this claim. The house itself, however, is undoubtedly old and very pleasing, the entrance to which, though extremely simple, is one of the best specimens of its kind in Charleston. A little farther up Meeting Street is the Nathaniel Russell House (now a convent) before referred to; and still farther on, at the corner of Meeting and Tradd, with its quaint Venetian porch extending over the sidewalk, is one of the former abodes of the celebrated Mrs. Daniel Horry (pronounced O-ree), of French Santee, one of whose friends was no less a person than Gen. Francis Marion himself. In fact, tradition says that it was from the window of this house that General Marion made his famous jump; but tradition is again in error, though there is no doubt of the fact that he narrowly escaped capture by the British at Hampton, Mrs. Horry's rice plantation on the South Santee. This residence of Mrs. Horry's is said to have been built about 1790, and the date is probably accurate enough, for in the *Charleston Gazette*, of April 23, 1787, there is an account of the burning of Mrs. Daniel Horry's residence of Broad,

which catastrophe must have led to the building of the Meeting Street house. All the walls in it are of painted wood, paneled, presumably cypress. The hall, which is divided into two parts by a central arch, separates the lower floor into two suites, and the staircase, which is in two flights, leads to the more elaborate upper hallway, which, in turn, leads to where formerly the drawing room lay, the partitions of which have been removed. The pediments to the doors, the cornice, and other decorative woodwork are all exceedingly good, though simple; and the quaint old kitchen, washrooms, and servants' quarters, together with the bricked court yard—cut off from the view of passers-by by a high brick wall—are typical of the domestic habits of the period the old house represents.

Following Meeting Street to the north after leaving the Horry House, one soon finds one's self within the sacred shadow of St. Michael's, which, by the way, is best seen when coming down Meeting Street toward the Battery, on a moonlight night when the mellow

Veranda Entrance
HOUSE IN CHARLESTON, SOUTH CAROLINA

Front
BREWTON SLAVE QUARTERS, CHARLESTON

whiteness of its tower melts into the luminous softness of the sky, casting the while a vivid shadow on the street below.

From St. Michael's corner, looking down Broad Street toward East Bay, one has an excellent view of the old Custom House, completed in 1771, which is one of the well-known Colonial buildings of America. The Commissioners of the Province of South Carolina signed articles of agreement with Peter and John Horlbeck for the erection of an *Exchange and Custom House and a new "Watch House"* in 1767, and the Horlbeck brothers left at once for England to obtain materials for its erection. The building was completed in 1771, the Horlbecks receiving in payment 241,740 pounds currency [*sic*]. When completed it became the general business mart of Charleston, and so continued for many years. During the occupation of the city by the British, its lower floors were used as a prison, and in one of the rooms Col. Isaac Hayne was confined and thence taken to execution. Afterwards the vaults were used as vendue stores, until the building of the present Vendue Range, and the rest of the building as post office and custom house. The situation becoming unsafe in the late war, it was deserted, and fell almost

Side View
BREWTON SLAVE QUARTERS, CHARLESTON

Side View
BREWTON SLAVE QUARTERS, CHARLESTON

Veranda Window Opening
BULL-PRINGLE HOUSE, CHARLESTON

steps of the Exchange as long as Charleston remained the capital of the state. On December 14, 1899, the 117th anniversary of the evacuation of Charleston by the British, the Society of the Sons of the Revolution placed a bronze plate on the western wall recording the many historic incidents of the location. The building is now used by the U.S. Light-house Establishment.

Standing here on St. Michael's corner—where until 1723 stood St. Philip's Church[9] (a plain structure of black cypress on a brick foundation) when a new one of the same name was erected on the site where St. Philip's now stands—and looking toward the Battery on the south and the Bay toward the east, one has before him the whole of oldest Charleston, although, strange to say, the very oldest structure in this city—an antique powder-magazine, built by Sir Nathaniel Johnson, in 1703,[10] is far away on an obscure lot on Cumberland Street, where it was located—Cumberland Street being then a forest primeval—for the ex-

to ruin; but it was afterwards repaired and the post office reestablished in it.

The front was originally on the east side, and wings extended out on East Bay, but as these obstructed the street they were taken down and the front changed to the western side. More recently, the roof being much out of repair, the cupola (see rough sketch, from the tower of St. Michael's Church) and some of the ornamental work were removed, but the building still presents an imposing appearance, and its historic associations make it an object of much interest. The Governors of South Carolina were proclaimed from the

RHETT HOUSE, HASSELL STREET, CHARLESTON[8]

[8] RHETT HOUSE—This house, on Hassell Street, is one of the oldest residences in Charleston. Its first occupant was Col. William Rhett, one of the officers of the Lords Proprietors of South Carolina. Colonel Rhett is one of the heroes of Southern legend, for, in 1817, he captured the notorious Steed Bonnet and his pirate crew that had been for some time an unbearable nuisance.

[9] St. Philip's Parish was the first established in South Carolina. In 1751, the town was divided into two parishes, the second being called St. Michael's.

[10] This old Colonial relic a little older, perhaps, than the powder magazine at Williamsburg, built by Alexander Spotswood early in the eighteenth century, is a small brick building with four gables and a tiled roof. As early as 1770, an act was passed directing its disuse, but, the war coming on, powder was stored in it until the siege of Charleston in 1780. It was then abandoned and became private property, which it still is.

LORD WILLIAM CAMPBELL HOUSE, CHARLESTON

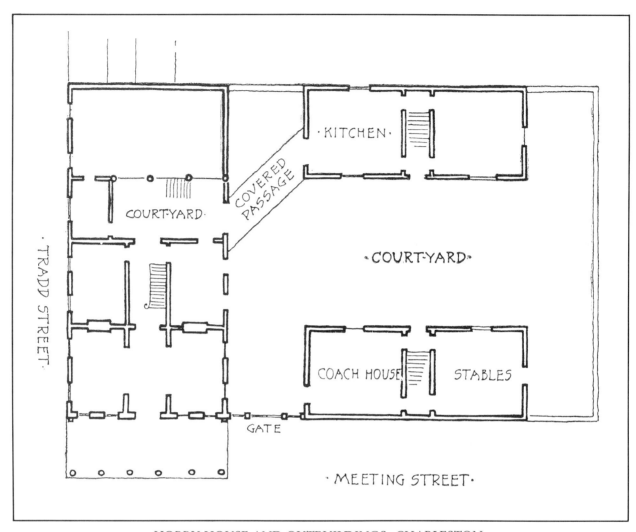

HORRY HOUSE AND OUTBUILDINGS, CHARLESTON

cellent reason that there it was out of harm's way. At the time of the Revolution, and prior to it, the land north of Broad Street was thinly settled as far as Hassell; but from there on it was open country with plantations scattered through it. The growth of the city in that direction must have immediately followed the Declaration of Independence, however, for Flynn's Church[11] (Second Presbyterian) fronting Wragg Square and occupying the highest point in the city, was built in 1811, and St. Paul's Church was completed in 1816,[12] and city churches are seldom placed elsewhere than in localities that are well populated and convenient.

As a matter of fact, all of Charleston is old, and the houses in the northern portion of the city, although

not Colonial, are almost invariably either modifications of the San Domingo idea, or specimens of the Greek Revival, as in the case of Ancrum House, on the

[12] ST. PAUL'S CHURCH, RADCLIFFEBORO—The congregation of St. Paul's was organized in 1810, under the Rev. Dr. Percy. They worshipped at first in the Huguenot Church, then unoccupied. The congregation was incorporated December 21, 1814, and the first Vestry elected in 1815. The cornerstone of the church was laid November 19, 1811, and the building consecrated March 28, 1816.

The style of its architecture is modern, with a Gothic tower; the front is adorned with a handsome portico, composed of four Doric columns supporting an angular pediment. This is the largest Episcopal church in the city; formerly it was furnished with the old-fashioned square pews, but these have been replaced by modern and very comfortable low pews, the effect of which is to add to the spacious appearance of the interior.

Dr. Percy was an English clergyman, who came first to Georgia in 1772 to take charge, as President, of the College which was established at Bethesda, ten miles from Savannah, by Whitfield. Whitfield bequeathed it to Lady Huntingdon, who appointed Dr. Percy to the Presidency and sent him to America with missionary instructions to officiate wherever he could collect an audience. It is said that while in Georgia he frequently preached in the fields under the shade of a tree. — *Guide Book*.

[11] FLYNN'S CHURCH—On May 16, 1806, the plan of Flynn's Church was placed before the building committee, by William Gordon, who was appointed to build it, and early in 1811 it was ready for purposes of worship. Although it was never finished the cost of building amounted to over $100,000.

·Slave Quarters of the
Horry House·
·Meeting St· Charleston S·C·

corner of Meeting and Charlotte streets, which, with its dignified Greek portico (to the side, of course, in deference to the European idea of what kind of a formal front a house should make to the street) and its high wall overgrown with a flowering vine inclosing a formal garden, needs but a touch of foreign color to change it into an Italian villa. Another and more ample monument to the Greek Revival, as conventionalized for domestic purposes, is furnished in the Witte residence on Rutledge Avenue, which was designed by an English architect, in 1810, for two English bachelors of Charleston. Neither of them lived in it, however, for the death of one caused the other to sell it immediately on its completion. The house stands with one end to the street in the midst of large grounds through a portion of which one must pass before reaching a position which affords a view of architectural beauties. The library and breakfast-room are the principal features of the ground floor where one enters; and the drawing room and dining room

the features of the second floor. The former chamber is most ornate, with an arched ceiling supported by fluted columns almost Byzantine in feeling. The staircase is quite circular and the second-story hall is decorated just below the frieze line with medallions in plaster showing studies of American game in cover.

This house is said to have cost a large sum of money which one can readily believe, for the plan is an ambitious one, and it was erected at a period when, having recovered from the ravages of the Revolutionary War, the town and state had entered on the period of their greatest prosperity. With the rich rice and cotton lands of Carolina yielding not only abundance, but wealth; with commerce on the high seas and trained slaves meeting every demand of domestic life, landowners naturally turned their attention to building both in town and country.

The post-Revolutionary, however, though regarded as the most picturesque period of Southern life because of the unique institutions that matured under it,

POWDER MAGAZINE, CHARLESTON,
SOUTH CAROLINA

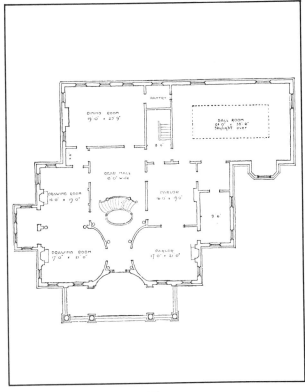

Plan
WITTE HOUSE, CHARLESTON,
SOUTH CAROLINA

and though it developed great fortunes such as that of Gen. Wade Hampton, of Columbia, who is said to have been the richest planter in the South and the owner of three thousand slaves — was no more brilliant socially than the pre-Revolutionary period, when European manners[13] and customs prevailed in Charleston, which rivaled every other American city in business activity, and surpassed most of them in domestic luxury. So much so that Josiah Quincy, of Massachusetts, who visited the city in 1773, wrote as follows in his *journal intime:* —

"This town [Charleston] makes the most beautiful appearance as you come up to it, and in many respects a magnificent. . . . I can only say in general that in grandeur, splendor of buildings, decorations, equipages, numbers, commerce, shipping, and indeed almost everything, it far surpasses all I ever saw or ever expect to see in America. . . .

"All seems at present to be trade, riches, magnificence and great state in everything; much gaiety and dissipation. . . . State and magnificence, the natural attendant on great riches, are conspicuous among the people. . . . There being but one chief place of trade, its increase is amazingly rapid. The stories you are everywhere told of the rise in the value of lands seem romantic; but I was assured that they were facts."

That Charleston should have taken rank as a social center of the New World at so early a period was

---

[13] FUNERAL CUSTOMS — Although most of the old customs are still honored in Charleston, that of serving refreshments at funerals is now obsolete. William G. Whilden, in his *Reminiscence,* speaking of the passing of cake and wine on such occasions, says:

"It was done with great solemnity. A cake called funeral cake was sometimes used, cut into blocks and iced all around. The custom arose probably early in the settlement of the country. The friends frequently had to come for miles (scattered as they were on their plantations), and to make a feast would have been out of place.

"On arriving at the house, the ladies were shown into one room; the gentlemen into another. The hats of the latter were taken charge of by a servant and turned over to ladies who were busily employed putting a band of crape around each and two streamers about three feet long from the back. A pair of black or white gloves were also distributed to each person. The ladies' bonnets were covered with black hoods, and a cape to cover the entire shoulders.

"A master of ceremonies, provided with a carefully prepared list, took a prominent position at the foot of the main stairway or elsewhere, called out the names at the door where the ladies were assembled in the order of their blood relationship; then the master of ceremonies called out the names of the gentlemen to escort the ladies, and so on till the assembled ladies were all provided for; the remaining attendants fell into twos, all walking through the streets, in the rear of the hearse or on the pavement, no one riding in a conveyance.

"At times the coffin was borne through the streets by the pallbearers, and no hearse used.

"At a funeral at the Scotch Church once, wine and cake were handed to those in the procession as they stood in Meeting Street, on the sidewalk. Some funerals were preceded through the streets by what were termed waiters (namely, two, four or six negro women dressed in white, with a black scarf over the shoulder reaching to the knees)."

Drawing Room
WITTE HOUSE, CHARLESTON, SOUTH CAROLINA

largely due to the fact that so many of the English colonists who settled it were Cavaliers, friends of the Lords Proprietors, with large means at their disposal; men who sought to reproduce in America, so far as could be done under different conditions, both the architecture and the social and domestic customs to which they were accustomed—and succeeded better than most of their contemporaries. These early colonists were enthusiastic builders, and but for the ravages of two wars, in both of which this historic city played a conspicuous part, numerous general conflagrations, and the earthquake of 1886, Charleston would have more high-class Georgian architecture to show than almost any other city in the United States. As it is, though the greater part of her most splendid buildings have been destroyed, what remains is often of a superior quality and in many instances uniquely interesting.

Entrance
HEYWOOD HOUSE, CHARLESTON

·Veranda Details· Corner of Meeting and Hudson Sts·
·Charleston· S·C· [1830]·

Simonton Gateway · Legare St · Charleston · S · C ·

A TYPICAL CHARLESTON HOUSE

A TYPICAL CHARLESTON VERANDA

HOLMES HOUSE — 1818–1822 — EAST BATTERY, CHARLESTON, SOUTH CAROLINA

Carriage Gateway
HOLMES HOUSE — 1818–1822 — EAST BATTERY, CHARLESTON, SOUTH CAROLINA

GIBBES (DRAYTON) HOUSE – 1780 – CHARLESTON, SOUTH CAROLINA

AUGUSTINE SMYTHE HOUSE, LÉGARE STREET, CHARLESTON, SOUTH CAROLINA

ANCRUM HOUSE — 1820 — MEETING AND CHARLOTTE STREETS, CHARLESTON,
SOUTH CAROLINA

WITTE HOUSE — 1810 — RUTLEDGE AVENUE, CHARLESTON, SOUTH CAROLINA

A GATEWAY IN CHARLESTON, SOUTH CAROLINA

Gate House

MANIGAULT PLACE, MEETING AND HUDSON STREETS, CHARLESTON,
SOUTH CAROLINA

Entrance

GEORGE EDMONDSON HOUSE, LéGARE STREET, CHARLESTON, SOUTH CAROLINA

Gates

GEORGE EDMONDSON HOUSE, LéGARE STREET, CHARLESTON, SOUTH CAROLINA

DE SAUSSURE GATEWAY, CHARLESTON, SOUTH CAROLINA

SIMONTON GATEWAY, CHARLESTON, SOUTH CAROLINA

Edmondson Gates · Legar

open·
ball·

marble above·

iron

wood

wood

wood
iron

iron

white marble

marble·

St· Charleston · S · C ·

·E·P·M· after measured drawings by·E·Eldon Deane·

a typical Charleston House
built about 1825.
on Meeting Street.

FLYNN'S PRESBYTERIAN CHURCH — 1811 — CHARLESTON, SOUTH CAROLINA

LILLYBRIDGE HOUSE, CORNER PERRY STREET AND ALBERT SQUARE, CHARLESTON, SOUTH CAROLINA

More Peculiarities of
Southern Colonial Architecture

Text by
Unknown Author
Originally published in 1902 as
Volume III of the Georgian Period

Entrance Gates
CHARLESTON, SOUTH CAROLINA

MORE PECULIARITIES OF SOUTHERN
COLONIAL ARCHITECTURE

IF one wished to embark on an interesting voyage of speculative inquiry, he might imagine that in the first ten years of the seventeenth century the ships of the world brought to this Western Hemisphere as many individuals as have entered this country during the last decade as immigrants, coming then, as they have come now, from as many and diversely situated civilizations, and then seek to discover what manner of civilization, what kinds of social customs, what forms of architectural surroundings would have resulted from the efforts of the motley horde of Huns, Italians, Poles, Jews, Armenians, Russians, Chinese, Japanese, Scandinavians, Germans, Irishmen and so on. The science of ethnology shows us how climate, social custom and family habit predicate the results of man's efforts, and on nothing is the effect of these more clearly stamped than on the architecture of a country. Fortunately, this country was, essentially, settled by Englishmen, and the ethnical characteristics of the American people do not vary much from those of the inhabitants of the British Islands, although there are parts of the country which bear the impress of the habits, customs and styles of building native to those early settlers of other than Anglo-Saxon origin.

But it could have made little difference at the time when the early settlers actually arrived what had been their home habits of life. They found themselves projected into a new world and they must house themselves either in natural caves or in some form of habitation that their own hands were capable of forming with most expedition, whether a wattled wigwam, a sod hut, a mud hovel or a log cabin. The log cabin was the natural selection of Englishmen, and from the log cabin was in time evolved, not only the present system of wooden dwellings, but one of the two kinds of building which are essentially American types. One of these types has already been referred to—the gambrel-roofed building. The second type that we are inclined to consider essentially American is the house with wing-pavilions[1] which is so characteristic of dwelling-houses in the Southern states, a type of dwelling that has sometimes been held to be one of the results of slavery, for, considered from this point of view, the wing-pavilion is but the slave quarter drawn nearer to the main house and occupied by the house-servants, and, finally, connected with it by open or closed galleries. But the wing-pavilion may have another derivation, and its germ is to be sought in the humblest type of dwelling, since it is in the dwellings of the lowly that changes occur least rapidly, and so there is more hope of finding still in existence the needed connecting links.

In all probability the log cabin of the South was very like the log cabin of the North, and its architectural form was of the simplest, and though the sun shone more fiercely in Virginia and South Carolina than it did in Massachusetts, we do not know that the Southern settlers undertook to provide a grateful shade on the outside of the cabin by giving a wide overhang to their roof timbers. But by the time that logs had been supplanted by slabs and sawed boards, we may feel pretty sure that this matter of providing shade had received attention and the householder had provided a place where his women-folk could work or sit under cover from the sun's rays, either by giving his main roof an overhang or by building a porch on the gable end. Now, as the original log cabins were essentially small structures of a single room or, if larger, of two rooms, it is plain that as the family increased more room was found needful, and, as log cabins are not easy to enlarge, it was the obvious thing to provide such enlargement in the shape of a second log cabin of the same size as the original, and, for convenience as

---

[1] The writer does not mean to suggest that wing-pavilion houses are not common in other countries, but merely that its development in this country was a natural one.

Modern Veranda
MEETING STREET AND THE BATTERY,
CHARLESTON, SOUTH CAROLINA

well as for sociability and mutual protection, it is equally obvious that the new structure should be built near the original with its walls parallel to those of the old cabin. These enlargements of the homestead were, in a sense, compulsory when it was needful to establish a son or daughter in a new home, and, as neighbors were few and doctors fewer, it was all the more desirable that the mother should have her daughter directly under her eye. Then, if the door of the original cabin, with its possible porch, was, say, in the east gable-wall, the demands of sociability evidently required that the door of the new cabin, with its possible porch, should be in the west gable-wall, so that mother and daughter might gossip with one another across the short space between the structures. This arrangement was satisfactory enough until it came time, perhaps, to provide a second daughter with a home, and then the problem presented was not so easy of solution, for if the new house were built in the same line over beyond the house of the eldest daughter, the new bride's door might as well be cut in one side as in another, since she would inevitably be ostracized from the family circle, as represented by "doorstep visits," while the mother would have to take twice as many steps in going to call on one daughter as she would when just running in to chat with the other. If, having this evil in mind, the head of the family ever thought to avoid it by building for his second daughter a cabin—always in the same right line—to the west (as we have assumed) of his own house, he doubtless perceived that, though the mother's steps might be saved, the new location would be as undesirable socially as the site at the other end of the second cabin. But being, doubtless, a man of resource, the father, after due thought, solved his problem in a way to remove all disagreeabilities, little

thinking that in doing so he was producing the germ of the second typical product of American architectural ingenuity.

He perceived that, although two of his daughters were off his hands and out of his house, really, the house itself was quite too small for his remaining and still growing family, although it would be amply large for the newly married couple; so he decided to abandon it to them and build a new and larger house for himself. This new and larger structure, being always guided by the instinct for convenience and sociability, he set in the space between the two cabins already built, but at right angles to them, with the gable end to the south, that is; setting it back so that its south gable-wall aligned with their north side-walls. The door of this new and larger structure naturally was cut in the south gable-wall, and in this way the doors, and possible porches, of the three dwellings fronted on a common, and small, door-yard. The mandates of sociability were perfectly observed; the mother in talking across to her eldest daughter need talk but half as loud as before, or in case of a visit need take but half as many steps. The natural passing to and fro between these three cabins inevitably, sooner or later, particularly after the grandchildren acquired locomotive capacity, suggested a platform of some kind, and, presently, a roof to that platform to give shade or protection from the weather. The result of this attempt to satisfy the natural demands of family sociability was the germ of the wing-pavilion house of the Southern states.

It may be asked, if this interesting type was evolved in just this way, why is it that the type is confined to the South and does not make its appearance in the North? And since it is a stranger in the North, is not this hypothetical evolution a little too fine-drawn to deserve respect? Possibly. Yet before waiving it aside as ridiculous, it is proper to attempt to answer the questions. In the first place, there was just as great a difference between the social instincts of the settlers North and South as there is between the climates of Massachusetts and South Carolina. The family life of the Puritan was far less expansive and joyous than that of the Southern immigrants, even if we take as a corresponding type the Huguenot, for here we have the asceticism due to sectarianism largely offset by the natural joyousness of the Gallic temperament. It seems fair to assume that a Puritan mother did not feel the need of doorstep gossip as keenly as did the mother living on the James or on the Santee, and no matter how much her New England descendants may now love to gossip "over the back fence," did not feel the hourly need of chit-chat that her livelier Southern contemporary may have felt.

SEA ISLAND COTTAGE, OFF THE COAST OF GEORGIA

Again, it must be remembered that the out-of-door life of the Southerner is longer by several months in the year than is that of the Northerner, and, while the latter might well hesitate to provide his wife and daughters with primitive covered verandas which would be fully serviceable only three months in the year, they were very reasonable things for a Southerner to provide, since they would surely be used nine months out of every twelve. Since we know that the most potent controlling influences affecting architectural forms are the ethnical and the climatic, we think that the absence of the wing-pavilion type in the North does not in any way invalidate the theory of evolution we suggest.

As a theory, and fanciful at that, all this may be very well, but is there any tangible evidence that can be adduced in support of it? We think there is.

The wing-pavilion house, as it exists in the manor houses of Maryland and Virginia, presents the type in its highest perfection, and just as it is difficult to determine of what nationality a genuine cosmopolite really is, so it is difficult in the case of these eighteenth-century houses, erected by men of great means, to decide whether the germ of their houseplan is to be looked for in this country or abroad; whether they here followed by one last step a process of evolution that had been going on about them and their ancestors ever since the country was first discovered, or whether

they adopted and simplified a type discoverable somewhere on the other side of the Atlantic. Types subsist longest in the lower stages of development, with inanimate things as much as with man, and in support of the theory of development here suggested we must seek for proof, not on the banks of the James, but in the back country of Virginia, Georgia and North and South Carolina, once held by the families of frontiersmen, and now occupied by small owners or renters of the land and by the white-trash, whose wants are simple and whose energies are commensurate with their means, who either live in the houses built by their

WAVERLY, NEAR COLUMBUS, MISSISSIPPI

J. T. CULYER HOUSE, PROSPECT HEIGHTS,
BROOKLYN, NEW YORK

more sturdy forebears or homes which they have blindly copied from those of their neighbors.

These small communal dwellings, a composite of three integral parts, are to be found scattered through the states named and in parts of Kentucky to this day, and surely present the simplest form of the wing-pavilion dwelling, which we hold to be the second significant development of American building.

The view of the Sea Island cottage—now occupied by negroes, but in all probability once the summer-house, or, possibly, the shooting-box, of the owner of some neighboring rice-plantation—shows the type described as it was treated late in the eighteenth century or as it might be treated now. The three doors front on the common veranda, and while the flanking cottages have become mere wing-pavilions of a single bedroom each, the central *corps de logis* has gained in size and comparative importance, though still consisting of but a single story.

It is interesting to study the varying manner in which the wing-pavilion is treated, for there is scarcely a possible combination of which an extant example cannot be found in brick or wood, from the group consisting of the main house flanked symmetrically by small independent structures wholly unconnected with it by gallery of any kind, whether covered or uncovered; to the group of two, the main building being connected with its smaller heighbor by an open covered gallery, as is the case at the Calhoun homestead; to the group of three where, as at Mount

Vernon, the wing-pavilions upon each side—independent structures—are connected with the main house by open, but covered, galleries. Then we find the single pavilion connected with the main house by an enclosed gallery, as at Acton, in Annapolis, and, again, the main house connected in the same way with a pavilion on either side, as at Lower Brandon. Little by little the gallery as a mere passageway gives place to a wider structure, constituted of one or more connecting rooms that serve also as a passageway, or to a passageway with rooms upon one side of it. Then pavilions, connecting rooms and main house are joined in one structure and covered by a single roof, as at Stratford House.

The last stage in the development of the wing-pavilion may be found in such a house as Waverly, near Columbus, in Mississippi, where the existence of the pavilion is not recognized at all in the roof plan, though the germ arrangement as it existed in the three log cabins is clearly recognizable in the plan of the front.

Climatic conditions as much as anything encouraged the development of this type of dwelling. Land was as cheap in the Northern states and families there liked as well as those in the South to have ample space to wander about in under cover, but the rigor of the winter months compelled the adoption of a more condensed house plan and the four-square rather than the elongated house was a natural result. The milder climate of the South made it a matter of indifference and sometimes a positive advantage that the rooms had such an expanse of outer wall enclosing them.

It is regrettable that more is not known of the men who actually designed the notable Southern houses—Homewood, Whitehall, Tulip Hill, Brandon and the many other interesting wing-pavilion brick houses of Maryland and Virginia, the houses that antedate the "white-pillared" houses of the Southern planter. These houses did not grow, Topsy-like. They are real architectural achievements, the final word in a discernible process of evolution. In some ways they are more lovable than any type of house we have: while having abundant dignity and elegance they seem intensely homelike, and though they have an old-world air and remind us that their indwellers belonged to a less eager generation than ours, they seem to tell us that beneath their silks and satins, behind their frilled shirt-fronts, beat hearts affected by very homely human emotions. One can imagine the men of that time treating their architects as Louis XIV treated his, that is, understandingly. There must have been both understanding and cordial cooperation to have wrought out structures so well composed, so refined in the intention of the detail—intention clearly, but,

SHEPHERD HOUSE—1830—LINWOOD, NEAR COLUMBUS, GEORGIA

alas, not always, in the South at least, refined as to the execution.

Climatic influences created two other peculiarities of Southern houses. Towards the end of the eighteenth century the early forms of heating-furnaces began to be introduced, and their installation required a cellar, but they could hardly have been the cause of the fact that a dug cellar was a more common necessity in the North than in the South. It is more probable that the necessity of storing fruit and vegetables safely away from the frost made cellars a necessity in New England, while the lack of such necessity and the fashions imported with West Indian immigrants, who had been habituated to having the air blow under their houses, made cellars in South Carolina, say, a comparative rarity. Be the secondary causes what they may, the primal ones—climatic influences—induced the Southerner very generally to abandon his lower story to the meaner domestic uses—to the kitchen, storeroom, rubbish-rooms, servants' rooms or what not, or, at least, to the occupancy of the men of the family, and make the rooms of the second story the scene of his domestic life. Thanks to this peculiarity, the houses of this particular period are made interesting by a great variety of exterior stairs, in single, double or treble runs, ascending to the veranda of the first story

SKETCH SHOWING RELATION OF THE
CHARLESTON ENTRANCE TO VERANDA FLOOR

OLD HOUSE, PARK AVENUE, NEW YORK

or to the generous porch at the same level, and as stairs imply posts and handrails, the fashion has provided us with many an admirable specimen of wrought iron-work. It is quite possible that hygienic considerations of a climatic kind had something to do with this abandoning of the ground floor to servile, in place of polite, uses. The houses where the *bel étage* is found at the second floor are most plentiful in the low rice-growing lands of South Carolina, Georgia and Louisiana, and very probably the custom was dictated by the prudential necessity of keeping the women and children of the family as much above the morning and evening mist-line as possible. It is this peculiarity that gives the houses of the period built in the far South an air very different from the houses built at the same time in Virginia and Maryland, which seem to suggest a hospitality if not of a more generous, at least of a more active, kind: it is clearly more easy to just step out of doors from the level to meet your guest than to take the trouble to run down a flight of steps, with the certainty that you must toil up them again in his company, so that one infers an apparent difference of cordiality between the greeting of the Virginia tobacco-grower and the South Carolina cotton-planter. Perhaps the latter's welcome was more dignified and stately, perhaps his advance to the head of his flight of steps had all the value of the advance of a feudal lord to the edge of his dais. But of one thing we may feel sure — both host and guest speedily retreated to the shadiest spot on the wide veranda.

The veranda of the Southern house is now its distinctive feature, and its development, which is easy to

trace, is clearly the satisfaction of a climatic necessity. The veranda, piazza, gallery, call it what you will, is worked into the house-plan so obviously as a necessity that one does not seem to be offended in the later buildings by the general practice of cutting athwart a great Classic order with the floor and balustrade of the second-story veranda. An order treated in this way in the North would surely attract adverse criticism, and even in those cases where a formless order of square posts has been made to support a piazza floor at mid-height, as in the case of the old Culyer House on Prospect Heights, Brooklyn, one cannot but suspect that the house was originally built by, or for, some Southerner who, tired of plantation isolation, had migrated nearer to the haunts of his fellow-men, and not knowing that their climate had induced in them different habits, or else willfully clinging to his own, made his architect surround his dwelling-place with two-storied galleries. These great houses with Classic orders, these real "white-pillared houses of the South," are very largely the product of the Greek Revival — as is the old house on Park Avenue, New York, whose important second-story doorway has a hint of Southern suggestiveness about it — and belong to a later time than the period here considered. But they merely amplified and clothed with new graces a type of structure already very fully developed; then, too, they are so very architectural in their composition that for us they lack in great degree the interest and charm of the earlier structures from which they developed.

The peculiarity of the Charleston veranda has been referred to in a preceding chapter, and explanation made that the doorway in the screen-wall gave upon the steps leading to the lower veranda and not into the vestibule of the house. It would seem that this arrangement must furnish a very perfect dust-hole for the gathering of all the leaves that fall and all the dust and straws that float about; but there is an obvious need in a climate where open windows at night are the rule that, in a city, a too easy access to the veranda upon which windows open should not be afforded to the vagrant and pilfering negro and his tramping white brother. In the country, on the plantations, the same safeguard was not called for, and so we find open flights of steps ramping up to the house-door, which, being usually placed on the axis of the front, gives a balanced central feature to the composition, which is often of great dignity.

Mr. Waterhouse has elsewhere accounted for the porch, or portico, as a needed protection from the weather, which the native or acquired hospitality of the householder provided for his guest, and in the North, and in other countries, we have the porch treated in myriad interesting ways without ever losing

Early Type of Veranda
THE BRIARS, NEAR NATCHEZ, MISSISSIPPI

its character as being, first of all, a protection to the visitor as he lingers at the house-door. It has been deepened to afford greater shelter, and it has been widened so as to make room for seats upon each side; it has been roofed in sundry ways, and that roof has been supported in ways as various. Even when, as at Shirley, it was given a second story it still remained only a porch. The present generation at the North is so habituated to living in houses more or less surrounded by piazzas or verandas, these useful adjuncts of the dwelling-houses have been so widely introduced during the last generation or two in all parts of the country, they have become such a distinctive feature of American houses, that, doubtless, many feel that they are a species of native growth that sprang up in any part or all parts of the country at the same time. But the advent of the piazza as we know it today is a comparatively recent occurrence in the North. The verandas of the Vassal (Longfellow) House are a modern addition, and, though there are many beautiful porches in Salem, there are few verandas, and these mere abbreviations, like that of the Bertram House. It was only when social life in the Northern states had taken on an idler habit, and it had been discovered that the manner of life in the South during the heated term was dictated by sound common sense, that we decided to copy that feature of their dwellings that did so much to make life endurable during a hot spell. Then the veranda and the "piazza habit" were im-

ported bodily, for both the veranda and the habit were evolved and developed south of Mason and Dixon's line.

Shade was, of course, the first desideratum, and if the porch roof could have given all the shade that was needed there would probably have been no great outward difference between the houses of the different sections of the country, but as that was an impossibility it was a very natural thing to expand the porch laterally, first along the sides of the house most exposed to the sun, and later, as it was found that the veranda was a delightful place for the taking of gentle exercise on rainy days, all around the house.

Homewood, Tulip Hill, Whitehall, Westover, Shirley, Monticello, Arlington, Brandon and many other of the manor houses of Maryland and Virginia are content with porches or porticos. Berkeley combines the covered veranda in its simplest form with a two-story porch, while Mount Vernon, almost alone of its class in that latitude, is endowed with a real Southern veranda on the east front. More than this, Mount Vernon, in this same veranda, indulges in some very illiterate architectural forms, forms which Jefferson would not have countenanced if he had been called in as adviser, as he was at Lower Brandon—where, by the way, there is a very interesting example of illiteracy in the capitals of some of the porch columns which were restored "after the war." The ingenious local carpenter, finding himself quite unable to copy the Corin-

Late Type of Veranda
COLEMAN HOUSE — 1830 — MACON, GEORGIA
Shows effect of Greek Revival

thian caps which still existed on some of the columns, made his new caps by nailing about the shaft selected portions of the jig-sawed brackets (with their well-known barbaric forms and hideous countercurvatures) which he had been using in place of Classic modillions in repairing the cornice. The result is a triumph of ingenuity, and one feels as if the work might have been done by some Babylonian master-builder. Southern work is fertile in such displays of illiterate ingenuity. One would not so much mind the illiteracy, but the failure of the ingenious intention and the brutality of the workmanship are a constant disappointment and offense. The doorway of St. Mary's Male Academy at Norfolk is merely an extreme case of the result of degeneration in both the designer and the mechanic who carried out his design.

At Mount Vernon the square veranda posts rest on the floor of the veranda as if on a stylobate, and this treatment is the one that is most usually followed both North and South; but in the later instances of porticoed Southern mansions the designer has frequently used a full order and placed beneath his column a complete pedestal. This, when a balustrade is introduced between the pedestals, does not appear an unusual and, so, local treatment; but in many cases there

is no balustrade and then these pedestal-supported columns become characteristic of the Southern section of the country. A curious reversal of this practice, devised to the same end — to bring the veranda roof to the level of the second-story ceiling — is found in the Bertram House at Salem, Massachusetts, where between the capital and the cornice is interjected a mere square fragment of architrave and frieze. At the South the column is, as it were, lengthened below the base, while in this Northern case it is lengthened above the capital.

The Southerners have used posts and columns so often in providing the all-needful veranda that they have acquired much skill and a considerable ingenuity in their disposition and adjustment. But it is not so sure that there has been any particular or regular development in their treatment, for one of the very early houses shows a very perfect understanding of how columns may be used to produce an impressive and yet not over-stately and too architectural an effect. Until within eighteen months[2] there stood near Natchez, Mississippi, an extremely interesting house known as Concord, where we have great columns springing each

---

[2] Concord was burned in February, 1901.

Rear

PYATT HOUSE, GEORGETOWN, SOUTH CAROLINA

from its own foundation so that they appear the very outgrowth of the soil itself, and these great seeming monoliths support in one place merely the light wooden pediment-fronted gable roof that overhangs, at two-story height, the twin stairs that ramp up to the veranda proper, while in others they support, in the main, merely the equally light roof that shades the veranda. Then, at the reëntrant angle where the porch joins the veranda, support to the roof at that point is given by naïvely using merely the upper half of one of these great columns, which here rests upon the outer wall of the lower story, which at this point is brought out to the face of the upper veranda floor. The curious thing is that this unorthodox disordering of Classic formulas not only looks entirely proper, but adds the needed touch of lightness to what would otherwise seem a rather ponderous treatment, and the lightening process is carried a step farther by the introduction in the intercolumniation of the great order of a smaller nondescript order of piazza posts.

Concord was the home of the last of the Spanish governors and was built in 1789, by one named Grandpré, so it is more than likely that the prototype of this interesting structure should be sought first in the Spanish West Indies, but in what direction after-

wards to take the next step backwards we hardly knew. But taken as it stands, or stood for so many years, it seems almost an ideal solution of the problem. It is at once simple and yet abundantly dignified and has, moreover, as suggested above, something of grace and lightness: its thick walls promise an equable temperature within, while the projecting roofs and not too large windows assure relief from the overpowering brilliancy of a Southern summer's day. The use of jointed drainpipe for downspouts recalls the use of similar pipe for the same purpose in China and adds to the columnar interest of the building.

The last step in the evolution of the veranda, or perhaps more properly the first, and final, step in its devolution, was due to the gregarious instincts and social needs of the householder. The open veranda is all right during most of the year, but there are seasons when one's guests are more comfortable within walls, and there seem to be many cases where the owner has decided that a satisfactory ballroom — that essential feature of the house of a Southern gentleman — or a banqueting hall, would be of more use to him than a veranda; and so we have houses whose interior accommodation has been increased by enclosing a veranda, as in the case of the Pyatt House at Georgetown, or the

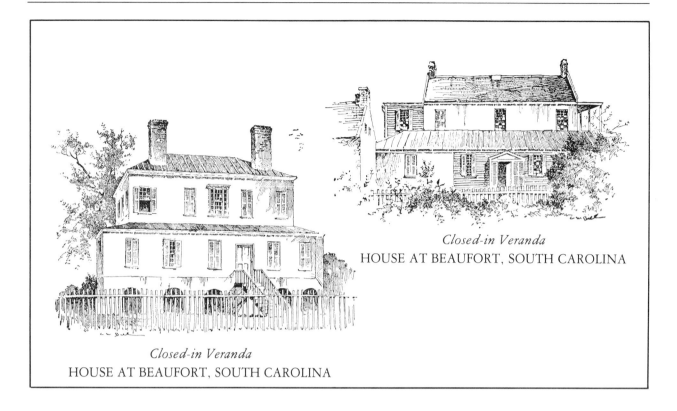

Closed-in Veranda
HOUSE AT BEAUFORT, SOUTH CAROLINA

Closed-in Veranda
HOUSE AT BEAUFORT, SOUTH CAROLINA

house at Beaufort shown by the annexed cut, where the line between the original veranda floor and the later tabby-built wall above is clearly to be seen. And there is another curious old house in the same place which shows how, as the family membership increases, verandas, which both downstairs and up, were originally but idling and cooling-off places, may be economically converted to the more prosaic uses of dressing, nursing and sleeping.

There is indisputably a difference between Northern and Southern work, both in the refinement of detail and perfection of workmanship, and it is all in favor of the Northern work. For this difference there must be a reason, and perhaps it is this: To this day, and quite apart from the efforts of poets and prose writers who have erected, if the term be admissible, the hearth into a shibboleth, the fireplace at the North is the center of home life and its enframement a matter of concern and interest to all members of a household. It is natural, then, that as the family has this feature close before its eyes at those brooding times when one seeks rest and comfort before it, the skill and the ingenuity of the selected designer should have been called on to make this household shrine more and more refined. This done, the natural sense of "keeping" led to the radiating of the same refining influence, first through the room, then through the entire interior of

the house, and, finally, over the exterior, and here, as the doorway is the chief exterior feature, a similar refinement centered mainly in the porch.

At the South, climatic conditions made the gathering-place where the family sought rest and comfort, not the heat-radiating fireplace, but rather the cool external veranda, and it happens that in the use of this household shrine the eye was habitually turned away from its constructive features and looked outward to the charms of nature, and, so, the work of the designer distinctly had the cold shoulder turned to it, and its inaccuracies, discrepancies and the coarseness of its details escaped a correcting observation. Even in approaching the house the veranda was observed merely as one of the large parts of the external whole and the owner was more anxious to reach its refreshing shade than to spend time in considering its lack of correct and refined detail. We think that climatic influences alone may be enough to account for the greater refinement and delicacy of detail in Northern Colonial work, just as they explain why the outside of the Southern building and its more generous plan received a greater consideration from the owner and his designer there, who knew that a large part of the family's time was to be spent outside of it, and, hence, it was desirable to give to the generous plan as agreeable an external expression as possible.

Doorway
ST. MARY'S MALE ACADEMY — 1825 — HOLT STREET, NORFOLK, VIRGINIA

CONCORD — 1789 — NEAR NATCHEZ, MISSISSIPPI

BERTRAM HOUSE FOR AGED MEN, SALEM, MASSACHUSETTS

PYATT HOUSE, GEORGETOWN, SOUTH CAROLINA

PRINCE GEORGE'S CHURCH, GEORGETOWN, SOUTH CAROLINA

SCALE·FOR·DETAILS

·FIRST·F
SCALE
FOR·PLA

DETAIL·OF·CORNER   ·F R O N T · E

T H E · B R I

·A N N A P O L I S